ABOUT THE HOLY SPIRIT

About
the
Holy
Spirit

FRANCISCA JAVIERA DEL VALLE

 Scepter

First published in 1932 in Spain as *Decenario del Espiritu Santo.*

Previously published in English translation by
Four Courts Press Ltd., Dublin, Ireland, and
Lumen Christi Press, Houston, Texas.
Translation copyright © 1981 Lumen Christi Press

Nihil Obstat	Stephen J. Greene, Censor Deputatus
Imprimi Potest	Dermot, Archbishop of Dublin
	March 16, 1981

The Nihil Obstat and Imprimi Potest are a declaration that a book or publication is considered to be free from doctrinal or moral error. This declaration does not imply aproval of, or agreement with, the contents, opinions, or statements expressed.

The Preface in this edition derives from that by Florentino Perez Ernbid in the third Spanish edition (Madrid: Ediciones Rialp, 1972) and includes an excerpt from Marcelino Gonzalez's life of the Servant of God, Francisca Javiera (second edition, Valladolid, 1942).

This edition copyright © 1998 by
Scepter Publishers, Inc.,
New York, N.Y.
www.scepterpublishers.org

ISBN 1–889334–11–1 (pb)
THIRD PRINTING / JANUARY 2007

Printed in the United States of America

CONTENTS

PREFACE

Francisca Javiera del Valle was born on December 3, 1856, in Carrión de los Condes, in Spain. There she lived all her life as a poor dressmaker, and there she died at the age of seventy-three, on January 29, 1930, in the Carmelite convent.

In her life we find three distinct periods. Up to the age of twenty-four she lived a life like that of any other poor girl in a Spanish town in the latter part of the nineteenth century. From 1880 to 1918 she worked generously and with a great spirit of sacrifice for the Jesuit Fathers in their dressmaking workshop attached successively to the Sacred Heart School, the novitiate and finally to the Apostolic School, all three located in Carrión de los Condes. These were long years of dull work and external monotony, often filled with humiliations and sufferings, but intermingled in a habitual way with great joys and pleasures of an interior life as rich in sublime interior experiences as in exterior naturalness and silent hard work. It was during this period that Francisca Javiera del Valle wrote, under obedience, the greater part of her numerous works, and certainly the most important.

Toward the end of her life, when she was over sixty and had retired from the dressmaking workshop, having lost—in silence—even her sewing machine, she decided to go to Mexico with a group of Sisters of the Cross, who were returning to their country during the height of the persecution there. But these sisters set out without her. Then she thought of going with other Mexican nuns, the Jeronomites of the Conception. Finally, however, she remained in her hometown, cultivating a little plot of land (which she rented) to make a living, and adopting no form of religious life in the canonical sense.

If the accounts given by Francisca Javiera del Valle of the constant mystical phenomena that she experienced in her spiritual life are ever published properly and in their entirety, then the science of theology will gain an extremely significant document. For they testify to ecstasies, visions, mystical conversations and raptures, repeated innumerable times; and they testify above all to the habitual and silent practice of heroic virtue.

Her writings can be divided into two clearly distinct types. The first and more numerous of these were written for her spiritual director. They tell of the supernatural experiences her soul underwent, and of the tests and consolations she experienced in the practice of holiness. In these she wrote of the Blessed Trinity; the Blessed Virgin and St. Joseph; of the virtues of obedience, humility, conquest of self and fear of the Lord; of the punishment inflicted on the angels; of temptations; the Holy Eucharist; the ways, joys, and friendships of God; the distinction between good and bad spirits; and many other subjects relating to God and the spiritual life.

The second type of writing was directly intended to spread pious devotions and practices. It consists of *Silabario de la Escuela Divina (ABC's of the Divine School)* and the present work, written in the form of devotions for the ten days before Pentecost and published now in English as *About the Holy Spirit.*

The first of these, as yet unpublished, is dedicated to souls aspiring to perfection. It aims to help them so that the many who set out on the way to holiness may also follow it to the end. For this purpose she describes the Holy Spirit as the Teacher in this divine school. She describes his lessons, and in general develops the same doctrines as in this "Ten Day Devotion," part of which is there repeated.

Decenario del Espiritu Santo was first published in Salamanca in 1932. Since 1954 it has been reissued a number of times in an edition that faithfully and deliberately retained certain irregularities of grammar and punctuation, but with a few slight modifications of a typographical nature, which were essential in order to make it more readable and easier to use as a book of devotions.

The greatest testimony to the value of this book is found in the report written in 1951 by Dr. D. Francisco Roldán for His Eminence Cardinal Almaraz, Archbishop of Seville, who knew and greatly esteemed Francisca Javiera del Valle. Portions of Dr. Roldán's report follow:

"This is indeed an uncommon book, not only on account of the subject matter of which it treats and the highest speculative and practical theology which it contains, but principally on account of the form in which this sublime subject matter is expounded.

"The highest speculative and practical theology, we repeat, because if the theology of the Blessed Trinity is at the height of theological science, then certainly a penetration into the intimate life of the divine Persons and an examination of their respective operations represents the highest point of that heavenly science.

"And in fact this intimate life and these respective operations of the divine Persons are here treated with such intelligence, with such subtlety, with such prudence and propriety, that the most learned theologian, far from finding anything reprehensible as regards Catholic dogma, will be forced to acknowledge the healthy and profound doctrine expounded. In support of this, we cite only by way of example the proposition chosen for the first day's consideration, which at first sight may seem strange: 'How much we creatures ought to love the Holy Spirit because he is, as it were, the motivator of our existence and the cause of our having been created to enjoy for eternity the same joys as God himself.' If one examines how admirably it is expounded, we believe that our humble judgment will seem to be correct.

"And as regards the practical theology, the science of salvation and sanctification, in truth there are no surer ways nor more direct, nor any freer from all deceit, than those which are here pointed out for reaching the highest Christian sanctity.

"But although the subject matter is so lofty, what distinguishes the book most from any other, even those treating of the same subjects as these here treated, is the form in which sublime subject matter is expounded.

"For however little of this book one may read, it soon becomes clear that it is not written by the theologian, who treats of the intimate life of God and of the intimate ways of the soul in its sanctification as things seen from outside, as a dry study or as scientific speculation, but by a soul which has learned this highest of sciences by experiencing and feeling it in the supreme school of the divine Spirit who is, after all, the Teacher whom the author of this book proposes to her readers, to lead them to the highest sanctity, which is the life of the purest divine love, love not for the sake of the temporal or even spiritual favors with which the divine goodness can enrich us, nor even for the sake of grace or virtue or even glory, nor for the sake of the joys that communication with God brings with it, but the purest love of all: love for the sake of love.

"And in this school of divine love souls are led along paths so secret but at the same time so sure and direct; the dangers that may be met on the way to this pure love are set out so clearly; the efforts the devil makes against the work of our sanctification are made so patent to us, that it causes wonder and amazement.

"However, all of this is expounded with such simplicity, with such sincerity, with such gentleness and divine persuasion, that we are subdued, and we see that the author feels what she says and that she says it precisely because she has felt it.

"Finally, although this observation is very secondary to our purpose, the language is pure, the diction is strong and clear, and generally most elegant.

"We end, then, by saying that it is our humble opinion that this book, as regards both the matter and the form, would not be unworthy to be placed beside the best writings of our most renowned mystics, St. John of the Cross and St. Teresa of Ávila."

The book is divided into sections that follow the ten days of the devotion. The Preliminary Remarks point out the dispositions that the soul should have every day when beginning the acts. Under the heading The First Day are grouped in order all the acts that compose the daily practice of the devotion. On the second and following days the same Act of Contrition, Opening Prayer, Litany and Concluding Prayer are to be repeated, while the Consideration and the Offering change from day to day.

Of course the book can also be used, and with great benefit, for ordinary spiritual reading.

Many souls, several of them very saintly and some exceptionally eminent, have reaped fruits of great blessings from a meditative reading of this book. May the Holy Spirit, the "Great Unknown," grant that it may continue to be a consolation, a stimulus and an encouragement, and that vocations to holiness may multiply without limit among Christians in all walks of life throughout the world.

DEDICATION

To the divine Essence, one true God, I dedicate this little book of devotions, to honor the three distinct Persons who exist in you, who by nature are in you and are called the Father, the Son, and the Holy Spirit.

The three Persons are God, but the fact that the three are God does not mean that there are three gods. The three are the one and only God, whom I adore, love, praise, glorify, exalt and bless. I serve, worship and pay all the homage I owe to my God, Lord and Master, acknowledging in the three distinct Persons the only God whom I must serve, for the three distinct Persons are the one divine Essence.

My only Lord and Master! When faced with your greatness it seems only just that I should not dare to move but should tremble with fear and respect. But although I wish to adopt this attitude, nevertheless I feel coming to life in the innermost parts of my soul the love of a child for the most true and most loving Father of all fathers. And this, far from frightening me, fills me with such a vast confidence in you that I can find nothing great enough to compare with this great confidence.

Now, most loving Father, as a child speaks and asks, so I want to tell you, most sweet and lovable Father, the great sorrow my heart feels and the ardent desire that my soul has cherished for so many years. My sorrow is that the third Person, whom we all call the Holy Spirit, is not known; and my ardent desire is that all men should know him, because he is unknown even to those who serve you and are consecrated to you.

Send him to the world again, most loving Father, for the world does not know him. Send him as a light to enlighten the minds of all men; send him as a fire and the world will be renewed.

Come, holy and divine Spirit! Come as light and enlighten us all. Come as fire and set all hearts aflame, that they may all burn with divine love. Come, make all men know you, that they may all know and love the one true God, for you are the only thing worth loving. Come, holy and divine Spirit. Come as a tongue and teach us to praise God unceasingly. Come as a cloud and enfold us all in your protection and aid. Come as plentiful rain and quench in us all the fires of our passions. Come as the sun and as soft rays of light to warm us, so that those virtues, which you yourself planted in us on the day we were reborn in the waters of baptism, may blossom forth. Come as life-giving water and quench the thirst for pleasure that occupies all hearts. Come as a Teacher and teach us all your divine doctrines, and never leave us until we leave behind our ignorance and coarseness. Come and never leave us until we are in possession of everything your infinite goodness wished to bestow on us before we came to be, when you were so eager to bring us into existence.

Lead us to the possession of God through love in this life and then to that other possession of him that is to last for ever and ever. Amen.

Divine Essence, accept this book that I dedicate to you; let it be for the benefit of souls, a glorious aim, for in that you have your greatest honor and glory. And because you are God and infinite in kindness I ask you, Lord, to grant me the consolation of seeing you loved by me and by all creatures, in time and in eternity, and that your holy and divine Spirit may be known by all men.

PRELIMINARY REMARKS

1. My first remark is that, in writing this book of devotions—which I have dedicated to God, the divine Essence—my intention has been to write it and offer it as a proof of the affection, esteem and admiration I have for all those people who, with great eagerness of soul, desire nothing, seek nothing and wish nothing but to give pleasure and joy to God in all things and who wish, whatever it may cost, to sanctify themselves in order to ensure the possession of God for eternity. It is for those people that I have written this book.

2. Whenever I meet, see or speak to people who aspire to holiness but do not know the sure way that leads to it, my soul becomes sorrowful, and I suffer greatly on this account.

To help them to achieve what they aspire to with that ardent desire of their souls, I am going to tell them what was taught and given to me by a most wise Teacher, who is the source and fountain of all wisdom and knowledge.

He exercises his function as a Teacher in the center of our souls, and the object of all his teaching is to make us see what true holiness consists of, what ways and means we have to acquire it and to protect it once it is acquired.

It is most consoling to attend this school and see how we learn our lessons, however stupid we may be. There we feel full of vigor and strength to undertake without hesitation even the most difficult and exacting tasks, whatever it may cost to carry them out, and whatever we may meet on the way.

We can achieve all things, we can learn everything, with the help of this clever Teacher and the skillful way he has of teaching. How clearly he shows us the ruses and tricks of our enemies, and how he teaches us to overcome them! So, come and join this school, which means living an interior life, where you will learn to know yourself and to know God. And afterward, from your own experience, you will see that what I say is true in everything I am going to tell you in this book.

3. The day before you begin this ten-day devotion, which is the eve of the glorious Ascension of our divine Redeemer, you must prepare yourself, by making a firm resolution to live an interior life and, once you have begun, never again to abandon it.

Do not ask yourself how much this is going to cost you; look only at how much it is worth. It has always been true that what is worth a lot costs a lot. And what is the effort we put into knowing ourselves when we compare it with the great benefits we derive from it?

Oh, how glorious it is to die to ourselves and live only in God! We cannot even imagine what it is to live in God, what it is to be deified! Words cannot express it; we feel, we taste, we experience, we touch, we possess, but no word can express what all that means! However, let us not think about the joys that loving nothing but God brings. An eternity of joys is being even now prepared for us. To suffer in order to achieve those joys, we have only the present short life; so let us make the best of it and suffer now for Christ Jesus, our divine Redeemer, as much as we can. How much he had to suffer, and how dearly it cost him to love us, simply because he wanted to make us happy for the whole of eternity! So whatever it may cost our nature, let us sanctify our soul and give joy to God in all things. Amen.

Act of Contrition
REPEATED EACH DAY

O holy and divine Spirit, supreme goodness and burning love, who from all eternity ardently desired that beings should exist with whom you could share your own happiness and beauty, your riches and your glory; you have now created for yourself, with the divine power that as God you possess, those beings that you so much desired. And how have these creatures of yours responded to that infinite goodness that so much wished to ennoble, elevate and enrich them?

Oh, you are the only object of my love; whenever I open my ears for a moment to listen to your creatures speaking, I close them immediately, for it grieves me to have to listen to the outcries they utter against you, their Creator. Satan is waging an infernal campaign against you, but that is no reason why men would hate and blaspheme you or cease to praise and bless you and so obstruct the attainment of the end for which they were created.

O infinite goodness, you have no need whatever of us, for in yourself you have all. You are the source and fountain of all happiness and blessedness, of all bliss and greatness, of all richness and beauty, of all power and glory. We, your creatures, are and can be no more than you wished to make us; we can have nothing more than what you wish to bestow on us.

You are by your Essence supreme greatness, and we, poor creatures, are by our essence nothingness itself. If you, our God, were to leave us, we would die that instant, for we can have life only in you.

O supreme greatness, how can it be that, being who you are and loving us as you do, you are repaid with so much ingratitude!

Oh, that my heart could break into a thousand pieces with the pain, the sorrow and grief it feels! Oh, that the burning love it has for you could cause it to breathe its last sigh, so that my love for you would be the only cause of my death!

Give me, Lord, this love that I wish to have but have not. I ask it of you in the name of who you are, God infinite in goodness. Give me also your grace and your divine light so that I may come to know you and to know myself and that knowing you I may serve you and love you until the last moment of my life and may continue loving you afterward for ever and ever. Amen.

Opening Prayer
REPEATED EACH DAY

My Lord, the only true God, you have all the praise, honor and glory that are your due, as God, in your own three divine Persons, none of whom had any beginning nor any one of whom existed before another, because the three are the one divine Essence. The three Persons are in your nature itself, and it is they who give to your greatness and sovereignty the honor, glory, reverence and praise that are your due as God, because outside of yourself there is neither honor nor glory worthy of you.

Infinite greatness, tell me why it is you permit that the three Persons who exist in you should not be equally well known by your faithful. The Father is known; the Son is known; only the third Person, the Holy Spirit, is unknown!

Divine Essence, you gave us a Creator and a Redeemer, and you did so without limit or measure. Give us also in that same abundance a Person to sanctify us and bring us closer to you.

Give us your divine Spirit to conclude the work begun by the Father and continued by the Son. For the Person intended by you to conclude that work and bring it to fulfillment is your holy and divine Spirit.

Send him once again into the world, for the world does not know him. You know, my God and my all, that without him we can never possess you. But with him, I am convinced, we will be able to possess you through love in this life and to possess you truly for all eternity. Amen.

Consideration

On this first day let us consider how much we creatures ought to love the Holy Spirit, because he is, as it were, the motivator of our existence and the cause of our having been created to enjoy for eternity the same joys as God himself.

We know through faith that there is only one true God and that he neither had a beginning nor will have an end. And although there is only one God, there are in him three distinct Persons whom we call the Father, the Son and the Holy Spirit, and the three are only one God, the three being the one and the same divine Essence.

This divine Essence has several attributes. And since it is only one God, although there are three Persons in him, all three have and possess the same wisdom, the same goodness, the same love, the same mercy, the same power and the same justice.

Nevertheless, these three divine Persons have, as it were, distributed among them these divine attributes. The Father has, as something proper to himself and belonging to him, power and justice; the Son has wisdom and mercy;

the Holy Spirit, who proceeds from the Father and the Son, has love and goodness.

This God, thrice holy, is by nature the source of all happiness and joy, all blessedness and greatness, all power and glory. He alone is unique and without beginning. Everything else, which is not God, had a beginning, and everything that had a beginning is from God and depends for its existence on his will.

Everything in heaven and on earth, everything, absolutely everything, depends on his will. If he so wished, the heavens and all that is in them, the earth and every inhabitant on it, everything, at the very minute that he so wished, would all disappear and would all go back to the nothingness from which God produced it. Even if this happened, he himself would still retain and remain the same greatness and power, the same happiness, the same blessedness, joy and glory, the same strength and beauty as before; because outside of him, nothing, none of the things that exist, can add in the slightest to God's greatness, beauty, happiness, blessedness, power and glory. In fact, nothing can add to anything that he is, because he is the only thing that is, while we and everything else are just nothing.

Therefore, since he is who he is and what he is, and since outside of him there is nothing whatever that can add to his happiness, consider him there in those eternities of his existence, forever . . ., forever . . ., because those eternities were within him, and received their life from him, for it was he who shaped them in all his greatness, happiness, blessedness, beauty, glory and power, which no one can ever take from him, because no one but him really exists. He is life and the only one who lives with a life of his own, and since he is life, he can never die. His divine nature comprises and has within itself more happiness, blessedness, beauty, greatness and glory than the drops of water contained in all the seas, rivers and fountains in the world. And his divine nature is always like the honeycomb, pouring out from himself what is within him. It is like a fountain that is always full, for his spring is infinite and immense, and he gives out from himself immense riches of all the beauties contained within his own infinite goodness. And this infinite goodness is a divine attribute that the Holy Spirit has as something proper to him.

Consider him as if lacking something, because he has no one on whom he can bestow that joy and happiness that the divine Essence pours out from itself; for goodness is, by its very nature, communicative and wants to make as many as possible participate in what it has and possesses. And to whom can God give what he has, whom can he allow to share in what he possesses, if no one exists but himself?

Since the three distinct Persons whom the divine Essence has within itself are one and the same thing, one God, how then can the Holy Spirit satisfy his desire? What means will he use to satisfy this divine attribute?

Consider what he did, as we know it from his own teachings. With the attribute of goodness he prevailed on the other attributes in God so that all worked together (as they always do, since they are the natural property of the divine Essence) with the will and desire of God, to create with his power beings who, without being themselves gods, could share in his greatness, his beauty, his happiness, blessedness and glory. In fact, beings who could share in all those things that spring from the divine Essence, and who could enjoy them, while God is still as he is, that is to say, the only thing that is and that has no end and can never have an end. The will and approval of God accepted what his divine attributes asked of him, and so we see how the Holy Spirit is, as it were, the motivator of our existence and the cause of our having been created for so much happiness and joy.

But how are we to thank the Holy Spirit for this kindness if we do not know him?

I must confess that personally I never knew all this until my unforgettable Teacher himself taught it to me. How was I to thank the Holy Spirit for his kindness when I knew nothing of it? And this, Lord, is why my heart is so sad when I see that you are not known. How are you to be loved when you are not known? And how are you to be known as you are in yourself unless you make yourself known?

O holy and divine Spirit! O immense goodness and supreme love! You who are a boundless ocean of boundless glory and happiness were, so to speak, lacking something when you had no one with whom to share everything you had and have.

How badly we respond to such immense kindness! How little we appreciate the great favors which you, O holy and divine Spirit, have willed to give us with such liberality and generosity. Without limit or measure you give them, taking us into that immense ocean that exists in you, so that for all eternity we may be eternally happy with your own happiness. That we may be eternally blessed with your own blessedness. That we may be eternally beautiful in your divine eyes with your own beauty, and great with your own greatness over everything beautiful and great that exists in the heavens that you created solely for our pleasure and benefit.

How I wish I could travel all over the world and speak about you to men, so that they would come to see what you have given us for all eternity and would begin to love and serve you now in this present life.

O you, my Teacher, you who are my all, in all things! Once they possess you, if they are to have some sorrow, as they must in this life, then it will be the sorrow of not having known you and loved you alone.

O supreme goodness, come forward to meet us, and let all men know you, so that in this exile we may never walk without your company. O holy and divine Spirit, be the light that will show us the way through the unknown paths that lead to you. Be the wise Teacher who will take away our ignorance and indifference. Teach us, like a loving mother, to speak to the Lord when we are in his presence so that, taught by you in all things, we may not be found unworthy to enjoy what your infinite goodness has prepared for us, but may enjoy all that together with you yourself for ever and ever. Amen.

Litany of the Holy Spirit
REPEATED EACH DAY

Lord, *have mercy on us.*
Christ, *have mercy on us.*
Lord, *have mercy on us.*

God the Father of heaven, **have mercy on us.**
God the Son,
God the Holy Spirit,
Holy Trinity, one God,
Divine Essence, one true God,
Spirit of truth and wisdom,
Spirit of holiness and justice,
Spirit of understanding and counsel,
Spirit of love and joy,
Spirit of peace and patience,
Spirit of longanimity and meekness,
Spirit of benignity and goodness,
Love substantial of the Father and the Son,

Love and life of saintly souls,   **have mercy on us.**
Fire ever burning,
Living water to quench the thirst of hearts,

From all evil,   **deliver us, O Holy Spirit.**
From all impurity of soul and body,
From all gluttony and sensuality,
From all attachments to the things of the earth,
From all hypocrisy and pretense,
From all imperfections and deliberate faults,
From self-love and self-judgment,
From our own will,
From slander,
From deceiving our neighbors,
From our passions and disorderly appetites,
From our inattentiveness to your holy inspiration,
From despising little things,
From debauchery and malice,
From love of comfort and luxury,
From wishing to seek or desire anything other
    than you,
From everything that displeases you,

Most loving Father, forgive us.
Divine Word, have pity on us.
Holy and divine Spirit, leave us not until we are in the
    possession of the divine Essence, heaven of heavens.
Lamb of God, who takes away the sins of the world,
    send us the divine Consoler.
Lamb of God, who takes away the sins of the world,
    fill us with the gifts of your Spirit.
Lamb of God, who takes away the sins of the world,
    make the fruits of the Holy Spirit increase within us.
Come, O Holy Spirit, fill the hearts of your faithful
    and enkindle in them the fire of your love.

Send forth your Spirit and they will be created
and you will renew the face of the earth.

Let us pray: O God, who by the light of the Holy Spirit did instruct the hearts of the faithful, grant us in the same Spirit to be truly wise and ever rejoice in his consolation. Through Jesus Christ our Lord. Amen.

Offering

The offering we are going to make to the holy and divine Spirit on this first day is a firm, determined resolution that we will love God for what he is in himself and not for what he gives or promises us. That our love will be so generous and disinterested that we will be moved to love him neither by the virtue he gives nor by the graces he increases nor by the gifts he bestows nor by the beautiful fruits he brings nor by the sweetness and consolations with which he delights the soul. That we will love him not for the friendship and intimate relationship he has with those who seek him nor for the transformation he brings about in them nor for the divine character he bestows on them nor for the union or marriage he contracts with their soul. For none of these things we resolve to love him, but only for himself, who is heaven of heavens, the only existing thing worthy of being loved.

Oh, how gentle and refined he is in the way he loves those who love him with this generous and disinterested love! Such a passionate lover of his lovers is he, that the heavens he created as a reward for those who serve him appear to him to be little. So he decided that to those who loved him with a pure and disinterested love, he would give possession of himself through love in this life, making of these two loves one only, in such a way that they should love each other with one and the same love and on equal terms.

Oh, is there no limit to the infinite goodness he showers on us, his creatures! He has even given us his own love so that we can love him with it!

This is the love the Holy Spirit gives us, and this is the love with which God wishes to be loved and honored. Let us pray to the holy and divine Spirit for it, and let our prayer never cease until we obtain it.

Let us make a second resolution: to enter into ourselves and to uproot ruthlessly from our heart any affection we find there, great or small, for things or for creatures. And let us say with a firm determination: Lord, from today, as regards loving, I am going to live as if only you and I existed in the world, confident that the Holy Spirit will give me the grace I need to continue with my resolutions until I breathe my last. Amen.

Concluding Prayer
REPEATED EACH DAY

O holy and divine Spirit, by whom we were created for no other end than to enjoy God himself, his blessedness and, with him, his beauty and glory for ever and ever: you see that although you have called the whole human race to enjoy this blessedness, very few live with the dispositions that you require to attain it. You see too, O supreme holiness, O infinite goodness and love, that this is less out of malice than out of ignorance! They do not know you! If they knew you, they would not live in that way. The minds of men today are so darkened that they cannot know the truth of your existence.

Come, O holy and divine Spirit, come down on earth and enlighten the minds of all men. I assure you, O Lord, that with the clarity and beauty of your light, many minds will come to know, love and serve you. Lord, no one can resist the clarity of your light or the strength of your love: they will not hesitate.

Remember, O Lord, the case of that famous man at Damascus when you first established your Church. You see how he hated and persecuted the first Christians, putting them to death. Remember how furiously he rode out on his horse, communicating that fury to the horse itself and galloping headlong in search of Christians, to put to death as many as he could find.

And, O Lord, you see what happened! In spite of all his intentions, your light enlightened his blind and dark mind. You wounded him with the flame of your love and at once he recognized you. You told him who you were, and at once he followed you. He loved you, so that not even among the apostles have you had a more vigorous defender of your Person, your honor, your glory, your name, your Church and everything related to you.

He did everything he possibly could for you, and for you he gave his life. So you see, Lord, what he was willing to do for you once he got to know you, while before he knew you he was one of your greatest persecutors. Give then, Lord, and you can expect results!

You see, Lord, it is no easy thing to resist your light or your blows when you strike with love.

Come, Lord, and if with the brightness of your light the minds of men do not come to know you, then come as the fire that you are and set aflame all the hearts that exist on earth. I swear to you by everything you yourself are that if you do this, there is no one who will be able to resist the force of your love.

It is true, Lord, that stones are insensitive to fire. But bronze, although it is hard, can be melted! Lord, there are very few stones, for very few have deserted you once they have come to know you. The majority, and it is an immense majority, have never known you at all.

Infuse into all their hearts the fire of your divine love, and you will find them asking you the same question as your persecutor in Damascus: "Lord, what will you have me to do?"

O divine Teacher, only Consoler of the hearts that love you, look down today on all those who serve you in great sorrow at seeing you unloved because you are unknown. Come and console them, O divine Consoler, for they have forgotten themselves and neither want nor ask nor desire nor wish for anything other than you. You as light and you as fire, so that you may set the earth on fire from one end to the other. So that they may have the consolation in this life of seeing you known, loved and served by all creatures. So that your loving plans may be fulfilled in all men and that all of us who now exist on earth, together with those who are to exist between now and the end of the world, may all praise and bless you in your divine presence for ever and ever. Amen.

Consideration

Let us consider how much we became indebted to the Holy Spirit at the very moment God created man and how much we ought to love him on that account.

The divine Essence, God, was pleased that his divine attributes should prevail on him to re-create himself, as it were. So the Blessed Trinity formed a kind of council to decide on the best way of creating those beings so much desired by the divine attribute of infinite goodness. The three divine Persons, which the divine Essence has and possesses, then offered for the creation of man the attributes that each has as proper to himself. For the rest of creation, with the exception of man, the attribute of power alone was sufficient; but the creation of man brought into force all the divine attributes.

The three divine Persons were then, so to speak, in conference to plan the work of creation, and the divine Essence, God, surveyed, as it were, the whole of creation before he created it and saw it just as it is. He saw at a glance the rebellion of the fallen angel and how later he would seduce man. And yet the three divine Persons, who are in this thrice-holy God, offered in favor of man, whom they saw seduced, all their own attributes.

The divine Word offered himself as a remedy for the great misfortune that would be caused to man by his seduction, for it would cause him to fall away from the happy state in which the infinite goodness of the Holy Spirit intended to place him.

The wisdom of God, which resides in the Word, designed and planned the means to repair and remedy these great misfortunes. The means this attribute designed and planned were the three ways of reparation, punishment and renewed exaltation—reparation to the offended Creator, punishment for the rebellious and seditious angel, renewed exaltation for fallen man, because the mercy of the divine Word decided to raise him up from his fall to even greater heights.

This infinite and immense wisdom, which embraces all things, decided that, as a means of reparation, there should be a God-man who would make reparation. And there was no way of doing this other than that God should become man. For this purpose the divine Word, the same Person whose boundless wisdom had designed and planned all this, offered himself.

The divine Essence, God, accepted this offering made by the divine Word, the second Person of the blessed and august Trinity. With the acceptance it was decreed that God would become man, so that then there should be a God-man who would make reparation for the fault that the creature was going to commit against the Creator.

In this reparation man would find his pardon and the rebellious and seditious angel would find the greatest punishment that God in his infinite wisdom could devise to punish his pride and leave him humbled, confounded, dishonored, downtrodden and defeated forever. For God always chooses the remedy that befits the misfortune and punishes as befits the sin.

Although God saw all these things before the creation, there was no reluctance on his part. Not for an instant did he hesitate; instead, he went ahead with the creation of the angel and of man, so desired by the Holy Spirit. The holiness of God loves and wills everything that he sees to be good and just, and his will never fluctuates.

The creation desired by the attribute of his goodness, which resides in the Holy Spirit, was something holy. And infinite goodness (which is, as I have said, expansive and communicative) never leaves a good undone even if it will be repaid with ingratitude. It is impelled to act neither by interest nor esteem, for there is nothing whatever worthy of God outside of himself; he was impelled only by his desire to do good.

An impulse of his goodness, and nothing else, prompted him to create angels and men and the whole of this creation that we all see and admire; he created heaven for the angels and paradise on earth for men. Another impulse of his infinite mercy and love prompted him to become God-man in order to redeem created man and raise him up to even greater heights after his fall, with no benefit whatever to himself. God has no need whatever of us; it is we who need him for everything. He is always doing good, even when he is repaid with ingratitude; he is always loving, even when his love is not returned.

As soon as this holy and divine Spirit saw the means planned by the wisdom of the divine Word, he in his turn offered to bestow beauty and riches on the angel and on man, undeterred by their evil conduct. He saw clearly the bad use they would make of his gifts and he knew that they would use what he so generously gave them to rebel against himself, their Lord and Master.

O supreme goodness, how can it be that before you created us, you saw how badly you would be repaid by these creatures of yours whom you were going to bring forth from their nothingness and fill with eternal life by an act of your infinite power? You created angels and men to live with you and enjoy you for all eternity. In your desire to make us happy, you were not deterred by the angel's rebellion against you nor by man's disobedience nor by the ingratitude, contempt, sneers and insults that you would get from the rest of the human race.

You saw that the proposal and plan put forward to you

by your infinite goodness was something good, that it implied doing good. And in the face of the love and goodness of your divine attributes that give so much glory to the divine Essence and themselves take such a delight in doing good, nothing could deter you. You saw clearly the displeasing conduct of these beings whom you so wanted to enrich, but none of this deterred you.

At the very moment when the power of the Father brings them into being and forms them from the mud, with your divine breath you fill the soul that you have given them with life, and life immortal.

O divine action, how admirable you are and how your goodness and your love are worthy of being imitated by all who serve God and who strive to do as much good as they can!

You who are consecrated to the service of the Lord, consider how this divine Master teaches us to do good generously and disinterestedly, whether it be to a friend or to an enemy, someone near to us or a complete stranger, someone grateful or someone ungrateful. When we meet anyone, let us do all the good we can, for the love of him who created all things for us before we even existed.

Knowing that we were going to fall, even before we did so, he prepared the remedy for all our misfortunes and raised us up afterward to far greater heights. This indeed is goodness, mercy, love, and love supreme!

Come, O holy and divine Spirit; come and teach us to practice charity in God's way, that by doing so we may be able to glorify and give thanks to the divine Essence. How sad it is, O holy and divine Spirit, to think that we practice great charity and make great sacrifices, and yet because we do not know how to do so properly it neither glorifies you nor gains any benefit for ourselves. Because you, our God, take no pleasure in our deeds and sacrifices unless you find in them purity of intention. You want us always and in all things to act as children of the Father. But how are you to accept or find glory in anything we do or in any sacrifices we make without purity of intention, which means they are not done for you?

If our good deeds and sacrifices are to be acceptable, they must all be directed to the single end of pleasing you; they must be done out of love for you and for the good of souls. These last are your great concern. It is in them you find your greatest honor and your greatest glory. Although everything we do out of love for you is pleasing, those deeds done for the benefit and salvation of souls, these and these alone, you tell us, are for your greatest honor and your greatest glory.

This is the way you want us to act, so that we may always behave as children of the Father and as pupils of that great Teacher.

And certainly we have powerful motives for acting always in this manner! After all, from whom do we come? To whom are we going, and with whose help? To whom do we owe more than to him? Who loves us more than he? Who is more concerned for our temporal and eternal welfare? Who has sacrificed himself for us as he has?

So let us treat him as he treats us, and from today onward let every breath be for love of him, to please and give him joy in everything. Let us try to save souls, always to save souls, for this is the greatest honor and glory we can give him.

O holy and divine Spirit, we resolve from this day on to follow your teachings and the example you give us, so that, having begun to glorify God in this life, we may continue to do so for ever and ever. Amen.

Offering

Peace of soul: a disposition that is essential if the Holy Spirit is to dwell forever in us.

The Holy Spirit is a lover of quiet and repose, of that repose that the souls feels when it seeks and desires nothing but its God.

When the soul is habitually in this state of repose, and desires to know nothing but the will of God in order to fulfill it at once, then it enjoys constant peace. And when this peace is there, then the Holy Spirit comes to that soul and makes, as it were, his abode there; and he governs and gives orders and commands as one who feels at home. He orders and commands, and is at once obeyed.

But when we are restless and disturbed and allow this restlessness to make us lose our peace of soul, then the holy and divine Spirit is greatly saddened, not because anything bad happens to him, but because it happens to us. The Holy Spirit cannot live in a soul where peace does not dwell; once we lose our peace of soul, the Holy Spirit cannot dwell within us, because the holiness of God finds it impossible to live where there is no peace.

The soul without peace is, so to speak, incapable of hearing the voice of God or following his divine calling. That is why the Holy Spirit does not dwell where there is no peace, because this divine Spirit, who is always disposed to act, retreats in sadness and remains silent when he sees that the soul is not so disposed.

The Holy Spirit wants to dwell in our soul for the single purpose of directing, teaching, correcting and helping us, so that with his direction, teaching, correction and help we may act always and in all things for the greater honor and glory of God.

For this reason, each one of us may quite accurately and truthfully call the Holy Spirit the God who lives with us. And if peace does not always dwell in us, let us resolve today to lose everything else rather than lose the peace of our soul, which is absolutely essential if we are to have the habitual assistance of the Holy Spirit. With that assistance it is certain that we shall possess God through love in this life and possess him truly for the whole of eternity. Amen.

Consideration

Let us consider how our divine Redeemer teaches us to esteem and appreciate the Holy Spirit.

When the fallen angel looked at man, he saw how inferior in nature this creature was to himself, but nevertheless how much God loved him. So the moment the Lord punished the angel for his pride—by depriving him of all his grace and glory and casting him into the hell created at that moment for that purpose alone, because up to then it had not been created—Satan, twice satanic, seeing his own plight, thought of nothing but how he could cause man's downfall, simply because God loved him.

God had left this angel all the natural gifts that he had already bestowed on him, depriving him only of grace, glory and beauty, while leaving him all the others as a means of punishment. And all of these the fallen angel used as a means to see how he could destroy the pleasure he knew God took in man. And he decided to use all his wisdom, all his knowledge and all his power to seduce our mother Eve, as the weakest point.

He succeeded in seducing her, by getting her to fail God in the only commandment he had imposed on her. But he did not succeed in depriving God of the joy he got from loving and being loved by man. On this point Satan made a big mistake; he thought that if he seduced the first two human beings, Adam and Eve, God would punish them as he had punished him and that God would thus be deprived of the joy he got from loving and being loved by man.

The only result this had for Satan was that he was defeated a second time, for God did not punish man as he had hoped. On this point he was humiliated because the punishment God imposed on our first parents was merely temporal, while he condemned Satan for all eternity, world without end, for as long as God would continue to be God, which he is for ever . . . and ever.

God punished the angels forever, for eternity, because their sin was one of malice. He punished man only temporarily, because man did not sin out of malice, but because he was seduced.

How clearly we see here the immense mercy of God and how reluctant he is to punish us! We see how willing he is to give us the good things we have not merited and how slow he is to punish the evil we have done!

He gives us, out of pure goodness, and without any merit on our part, the very same joy that he himself enjoys and has in himself. And he gives it without limit or measure, while the punishment he imposes for the evil we do, he always limits and measures. For although the hell he created is indeed horrible, he does not necessarily send us there to punish us for our sins. He sees all the infidelity committed by the angel and by man before creating them, but he does not immediately determine the place where they are to be punished. Instead, he waits until they actually commit the infidelity, and only then does he determine it. But before they are created, he prepares for them everything that gives them pleasure, happiness and contentment, both temporal and eternal. And he fills the whole of creation with beauty, all for the benefit of the angel and man. He prepares all the beauty of creation before he creates them so that from the first instant of their existence they may be happy and contented.

My God, you are all goodness, all mercy, all love!

When Eve let herself be seduced and in turn seduced Adam, she did so without malice. When both were seduced, they failed in the one commandment God had imposed on them. As soon as the Lord spoke to them, showing them and reprimanding them for their fault, they were humiliated, they wept and they confessed their guilt.

Then the Lord, our God, turned to Satan and said: "I will raise them up from their fall to far greater heights."

When the divine Essence, as it were, surveyed the whole of creation before he had created it, the wisdom of God (which, as I have said, resides in the divine Word) saw how few souls would love and serve him faithfully. Then his immense and infinite wisdom decided that when the time came, and the two natures were united, these few souls who were faithful to their God would be gathered together, and from then on would be regarded by him no longer as creatures but as adopted children.

When the time laid down for the redemption of the human race arrived, the divine Word became man and the two natures were united. There then existed in the world a God who was at the same time man, and for thirty-three years a man who was God lived among men.

The men among whom this God-man lived offended against all truth and justice by condemning him to death. They placed him on the holy wood of the Cross, and no sooner was he crucified, than the blessed soul of that man, which was united to the divinity of the divine Word, began to discuss with God, his Father, the manner in which he wished to raise up man from his fall.

Consider the circumstances of this discussion. Crowned with thorns, bleeding from head to foot, his back torn to pieces, his hands and feet pierced with great nails, having no place to rest or even lay his head! And in that state the blessed soul of that God-man never for a moment ceased to ask and pray to his Father to grant him what he so wished for men. That blessed soul, burning with love for men, ardently desired that all men should be gathered together in him, so that he would be the body, the soul and the life of all those gathered in him.

And the divinity of the Word, to which this most holy humanity was united, transmitted to it its truth and wisdom. Then that blessed humanity, with the goodness and wisdom that the divine Word transmitted to it, since they are inseparably united, asked that the holy and divine Spirit be sent to men, so that all those gathered together in the Word could live with one body and one soul, and this new gathering would be directed and taught by the Holy Spirit. He also asked that once the Holy Spirit was in possession of this gathering, he would regard all those gathered there not as creatures of his but as children by adoption. They would be children adopted by the justice of God, to which overabundant reparation has been made by the God-made-man, by the mercy of the divine Word, which is united to the most holy humanity, and by the love and goodness of this holy and divine Spirit.

O most holy humanity, who but God alone can know how much you suffered during those three hours you were hanging on the Cross!

Forgetting the most painful state to which men reduced you, taking no account of your great sufferings, and never ceasing to pray and implore your heavenly Father to grant you the favor you were asking for the whole human race, you wanted to unite them all and make of them one body and soul. You remember the scene: all those people insulting you, scoffing and sneering at you, crying out against you, grievously offending against the justice of God! And you, my life and my all, what was your reaction to all this? You excused them, saying: "Father, forgive them, for they know not what they do," and you continued discussing and negotiating their eternal happiness! You prayed that your torments might be prolonged. You arranged that the holy and divine Spirit be sent to us, to teach, direct and govern us, because without the Holy Spirit man cannot be raised to the dignity to which you wish to raise him.

Let all souls consider the great torments he suffered. Consider the justice of God, in allowing Jesus Christ to bear the burden that we had merited, while he burned with desire to obtain from his heavenly Father what he so desired for our sake! The power of God, his Father, allows the divinity of Christ to be kept miraculously hidden from his humanity, so that the humanity gets no help from the divinity.

This terrible suffering will be understood by no one but those who have once tasted union with God and whom he has then left helpless and abandoned after they have been united with him. However, the torment that Christ suffered and the torment of those souls are less comparable than reality to shadow. But the moment this happens to them, we know that their heart breaks in two with pain and suffering.

So how great must those torments of Christ have been, there on the Cross, suffering such terrible pain, praying for the gift he so wished to obtain for us? And then came that abandonment by his divinity, which, we know, is more painful for souls than hell itself.

Consider the state of Christ's most blessed soul when it felt that abandonment. Up to that moment he had not uttered a cry in spite of all he had suffered. But now: "My God, my God, why hast thou forsaken me?" Look at Jesus Christ and see what a great price he has to pay. What he wants to obtain for us was that gift above all other gifts; but before being granted it, he has to go through suffering above all other sufferings. Consider, then, the price Christ had to pay to obtain the Holy Spirit for us from God!

He wanted to gather us all together in him, which means the establishment of his holy Church, and this could not subsist without the Holy Spirit. So he prolonged his life, which as God he could do, until he obtained the Holy Spirit for us from his Father.

The eternal Father granted his request, he established his Church and then immediately he spoke and said: "It is consummated."

O souls consecrated to the service of the Lord, let us learn from Jesus Christ, our divine Redeemer, how much we should esteem and appreciate the Holy Spirit.

Come, O holy and divine Spirit, come and satisfy the ardent desire of that man whom you formed in the virginal womb of Mary Immaculate and who, although in his sufferings he is man, is God in what he desires and prays for. He desires and prays for what the divine Word, to whom he is united, desired. Come down to us, as that God-man desired and prayed. Direct and govern us in all things, teach us to glorify you, so that beginning in this life, we may thus continue for ever and ever. Amen.

Offering

Prayer: for with what joy and happiness we overcome ourselves in all things through prayer, however difficult they may be and however hard we find it to overcome and mortify ourselves.

Consider how easy it is for a little bird to fly up into the high branches of leafy trees and to ascend to great heights, by means of the two wings that God gave him. Once his flight is over and he perches on the tree, how cheerfully he sings to show that flying makes him happy and joyful.

So also the mortified soul, just like the little bird, has wings with which to fly. Like the bird, it also perches in the tree and, once its flight is over, is cheerful and sings for joy.

Consider for a moment those souls who wish, seek and desire nothing whatever, neither in heaven nor on earth, but their God, with whom they are vitally in love. True, you will find few of these souls, but there are some, and there always will be until the end of the world.

Look at them, and you will see that when they want to mortify themselves, they make use of prayer and of their love of God. Like the bird, they soar to greater heights with the help of those two wings. With prayer and love of God, they ascend as on wings, above all created things, and they overcome and become masters of themselves. And when they reach the heights, they alight on Mount Calvary and there they gaze, as if the Cross were still there with our divine Redeemer, Jesus, nailed to it, like chaste doves cooing with the love of their loves, showing the beloved, whom they love with all their soul, that they are willing with great joy to mortify themselves whenever the occasion arises.

And the occasion does arise continually, because even when they can think of no more mortifications themselves, God permits and disposes that other creatures should present them with many opportunities. And whenever there is no creature to mortify them, then God, great as he is in all things, sees to it himself; thus showing the souls who wish to be his that mortification must be something continuous, like the beating of the heart.

Let us try to have the courage to practice this mortification, for we have nothing else to offer our lovable Jesus. And how ardently he desired to give his life for us! So let us say to him: Lord, I hunger and thirst to die to myself in all things and to live only in you so that, beginning in this life, I may so continue for ever and ever. Amen.

Consideration

Let us consider the school of the Holy Spirit, where he holds this school, how he runs it and what he teaches. For it is by practicing the teachings of the Holy Spirit that we achieve true holiness.

The Holy Spirit, our divine Teacher, holds his school within the souls of those who ask him and who really want to have him as their Teacher. That is where he does his work as a Teacher without making any noise or using any words, and he teaches the soul to die to itself in all things and to live only in God.

The method of teaching used by this most skillful Teacher is very consoling for us. The only place he is willing to hold his school and show us the ways that lead to true holiness is within our own soul, and he is so effective, so skillful in his teaching, so wise and masterly, so powerful and subtle, that, without knowing how or why, we feel completely changed shortly after beginning to attend the lessons in this school.

Before going to school, we had little ability, we were very ignorant and dull as regards understanding the things we heard preached. But once we attend this school, we learn everything quite easily, as if we were infused deep inside us with the knowledge and ability of the Teacher himself.

Words are not the medium he uses. He rarely speaks, and never at the beginning. If we really put into practice the lessons he teaches us, then he may speak, although little, just to show us that he is pleased. But the lesson has to be practiced properly, because in this school it is all a question of practicing what we are taught: if we do not practice it, the whole thing is finished, the school closes down, its doors are closed to us.

Although the school takes place in the center of our soul, nevertheless we cannot enter there unless the Teacher allows us. However much we may want to go in ourselves, we neither know the way nor have the ability. The only thing we can do in that case is to remain within ourselves without coming out, and stand at the door, sincerely lamenting and regretting our loss unselfishly. Generosity and unselfishness are, as it were, the touchstone of this school, for everything taught here must be practiced generously. Otherwise, nothing we do has any merit in the eyes of our Teacher.

At the beginning he says nothing but tolerates everything and does not punish us. For he is so loving and takes pity on us, seeing that we are ignorant, and he never demands or asks more than we can do.

The medium he uses to teach us is a bright and beautiful light that he shines on our understanding. When we are very careful to fulfill and practice the truths he teaches us, then in addition to this light in our understanding, he also gives a kind of impulse to our will. Then the will feels itself burning with love for its God and Lord, and it knows well when it receives this impulse that it has not merited it in any way, but has been given it. No one tells it this, but the soul understands and knows that it is so.

In this school we seem to breathe wisdom and knowledge, and all this wisdom and knowledge is directed toward knowing God and knowing ourselves. That is the foundation of everything we are taught. Until this is well grasped by the soul it cannot make any progress. The Teacher suspends all his lessons; and until this fact is well rooted in the soul, he does not go ahead with his teaching.

He tells us nothing about penance. Personally, I think

this is so because the soul of its own accord inclines more toward penance than toward mortification.[1] What we do see with one of those lights that he gives to the understanding is that penance alone, without mortification, will fill the heart with pride. Therefore we learn to do penance with great discretion, for we see with that light which comes from the divine Spirit that Satan is very active trying to get the soul to do great penances.

In dealing with the saints, Satan has one object. But in dealing with people who are imperfect, he has quite another: he inclines them to do penance while withdrawing them from mortification; for in penance, however continuous, he sees no danger. Penance alone does not sanctify, but continual mortification makes great saints. Through continual mortification we learn to die to ourselves in all things and we acquire pure love of God, without which we can have neither friendship nor union with him nor any transformation, for this is all done by love.

Through continual mortification we leave behind us our self-slavery and become masters of ourselves. Through continual mortification we arrive at the happy state in which our first parents were placed, and as a reward for continual mortification God gives himself to the soul in this life. In this school what we learn, and the objects of all the lessons, is precisely continual mortification.

There is a special lesson on fasting. It teaches us not to deprive the body of anything it needs but never to give the appetites what they want, desire or seek beyond necessity. When it is a question of necessity, it is the body that asks, and it asks simply for food and nothing more. But the appetites ask for luxury and comfort, for they are like capricious children who ask, never out of necessity, but merely out of whim and passing fancy.

[1] The author distinguishes penance (or practices of corporal mortification) from continual self-denial in little things.

Therefore this admirable Teacher encourages us above all else to deprive ourselves of luxury. And the soul, always mindful of the tragedy that occurred in paradise, willingly abstains from the fruit because it wishes to make reparation to God, if possible, for the fault committed by that unfortunate mother of ours, with whose blood we are now contaminated.

With all the training and all the lessons learned at this school, the soul begins to forget itself completely and to live with no other object in anything it does than to please God always and if possible to make him loved by all.

It forgets itself, thinking neither of acquiring virtues nor of advancing in virtue nor of meriting grace nor of reaching heaven nor of sanctifying itself. For itself and for other souls it wishes, desires and prays for nothing but to love God and, if it were possible, to love him as he deserves. Because the disinterested and unselfish love that is taught in this school is the love with which we must always love God; this is what the divine Teacher exhorts and teaches us to desire.

He shows us how to love God as he loves us. And why does God love us? For no reason, since we have nothing and can give him nothing; he loves us for the sake of loving us. So let us also love him simply for the sake of loving him. He wants to bestow on us his own eternal happiness and blessedness; and in creating us, the only purpose he had in mind was to create us for all that happiness and blessedness.

O holy and divine Spirit, you see that we are incapable of taking the right road to reach you. That unselfish love we owe to God our Lord and Master does not burn in our souls, and continual mortification is unknown to us; yet both these exercises are absolutely necessary for us to go to you.

O life of our life and soul of our soul, as the bird needs

his wings to fly, which is the purpose for which he was created, so we, O holy and divine Spirit, cannot fly to you, for we are without wings.

Come then, O holy and divine Spirit, come as a Teacher and show us from this day on how to practice that unselfish love. Set alight that fire of divine love in our soul, and there is no doubt that with it we shall then willingly undertake the practice of mortification.

Come, for if you come, it is certain that we shall achieve everything. We shall love you as we should and shall give you the consolation you so much desire: the consolation of being happy with you for ever and ever. Amen.

Offering
Mortification.

Mortification should be for anyone who aspires to holiness what breathing is for the body. Unless it breathes, the body cannot live; so our soul needs mortification if it is to attain the holiness it desires. My holiness will be in proportion to my mortification.

Holiness is very different from what many people think. Many people think a saint is someone who has ecstasies, raptures, visions and revelations, who enjoys heavenly sweetness, consolations and thousands of other things that the soul feels in the spiritual life.

But none of these things are necessary in order to attain holiness. Holiness is acquired through mortification and is perfected also through mortification. But God often gives a taste of these things to people who mortify themselves very much, as a reward for their continued effort. In this life continual mortification is purgatory for our rebellious nature, which already knows that we were created to have enjoyment.

We never reach the stage where mortification becomes easy. In other things we get into the habit, which makes them easy; but when it comes to mortifying and conquering ourselves in order to please God, we always find that difficult.

And it is as a reward for continually conquering itself in everything, for no other purpose than to please God, that he gives the soul these sweet things and consolations.

But look at those people, as you would look at yourself in a mirror, who always strive to be faithful to the Lord, and you will see how they weep and feel sorry and ashamed when he gives them a taste of these things. You will see that they use those very proofs of God's affection for them to persuade him not to give them any of these things.

Let us try, then, to imitate them in this respect and to mortify ourselves for no other purpose than to give pleasure to God and to show him in this way our pure and unselfish love, so that we will achieve love of God in this life and continue loving him afterward for ever and ever. Amen.

Consideration

Let us consider some important lessons that our most wise Teacher gives us. I call them important because they are so serious that if we fail to practice them, he will leave us and we shall be unable to achieve union with God.

The object of the lessons I am now referring to is that we should act toward all our neighbors without exception—whether they be friends or not or even if they are avowed enemies—as he acts toward us. He wants us to treat everyone equally, with the charity we learn from him who is such a wise, skillful, prudent, discreet, active, sweet and loving Teacher. He of course deserves all these titles because in these lessons he seems to want to transmit to us and impress on us all these same qualities.

He does not give us or show us or teach us these lessons by means of the light that I have already said he shines on our understanding. No; these go directly to the will, and he imprints and engraves them there in the most intimate part of our soul so that we will never forget them. And if we wish to show our gratitude for all these demonstrations of love and affection that this unforgettable Teacher gives us, we should receive and regard these teachings of his not as mere lessons but as commandments. Our will should accept them fully and we should put them into practice.

He teaches that we should speak and act always with great simplicity and that we should never treat or speak to anyone in a deceitful way for any reason whatsoever.

Simplicity, he says, is a characteristic proper to the

children of God, while deceit, or pretense, is proper to Satan and his followers. Remember that it was Satan who planted this seed, together with the seed of vanity, in the heart of the woman when he seduced her into committing the first sin. Also, the divine Teacher tells us that God so abhors anyone who treats his neighbor deceitfully that no such person will enter or enjoy rest in him.

He exhorts us that we should never deliberately commit any act, however slight, of this nature. And he urges us to give a special place in our heart, special appreciation and esteem, to those who, with their contradictions and opposition, give us opportunity to get rid of that attachment to our own free will.

He exhorts us to be demanding with ourselves, to direct our whole life toward virtue and perfection, while at the same time being tolerant of others. He instructs us to have great prudence in all things and to act with discretion and care because Satan, our common enemy, is always going among us sowing seeds of discord so that we will reap a harvest of disagreement, which is the fruit of the seeds he sows. And our Teacher shows us the many different ways in which Satan disguises himself.

One of the disguises he often uses is false zeal. For souls consecrated to the service of the Lord, this is the mask he uses to cover his face, and so he comes with appearances of great zeal. Remember that apart from the possession and vision of God, Satan kept all other faculties he had been given. The Holy Spirit gave him such a privileged intellect that with it he knew all virtue and perfection, although he did not want to practice them. That is why he is such a master in the art of seduction and deceit, using apparent or pretended virtues, for appearances and pretenses are all he has. Once he rebelled against God, all his knowledge and all his intelligence turned to deceiving, seducing, pretending and disguising, and now that occupies him completely. But we destroy all his knowledge, wisdom and power simply by following the truth, and in this way we leave him humiliated, confused and more and more defeated in his own pride.

The Holy Spirit insists again and again on how displeasing it is to God that we should treat or speak to our neighbor deceitfully. He forbids us to expose, manifest or express in any way whatever the weaknesses, imperfections, faults or sins of our neighbors. Our attitude to these things should be to speak of them only to God, to ask his grace and pardon for them.

He exhorts us strongly and energetically against spiritual envy. We should never let Satan seduce us into committing that sin, for anyone who commits it is a flagrant thief who robs God of the honor and glory that are his due and that it is our duty to give him. Far from committing that sin, we should rejoice with great joy whenever we see or hear others being praised. We should never be upset by petty pride or envy (as are some people who are far from perfect) when we hear others being praised or see them do some act of virtue. Our Teacher tells us that anyone who commits this sin is as if dominated by it and anything good he sees or hears about his neighbors hurts him as if he saw them committing great sins. Spiritual envy rots anyone who has it, right to his innermost parts, and his spiritual ruin is certain.

And I say that he tells us this most strongly, because even our senses seem to be affected by this lesson.

Another thing he tells us is that if ever we are persecuted, accused or reprehended with false zeal, we should maintain a rigorous silence in the face of it all and should open our heart, full of love and affection for those people, however often they try to hurt us, never giving the slightest sign of resentment. After all, in this way they help us very much to attain more easily the sanctification of our soul.

He also exhorts us very strongly not to offend or criticize any of our neighbors, because anyone who offends or criticizes another is far from being a saint.

He also urges us very forcefully to have great fear or mistrust, not of God, but of ourselves, whenever we are praised or complimented. The praise, honor and glory men give us are not due to us, but to God, since it is he who gives us everything we have, including all the things for which we are praised and complimented.

Satan, our common enemy, knows that he can do very little with the pupils who attend this school. First of all, it is impossible for him to get in there. Secondly, although he prowls around the walls listening, it is of no avail, for there is nothing to be heard; in this school everything happens in silence, quietness, rest and complete reserve.

The reserve we practice and exercise in this school is such that everything the soul learns there remains engraved and concealed in the center of the soul, so that neither Satan nor creatures know anything of it. A kind of natural reserve is given to cover up everything the soul learns or receives, as if a lock were put on it to forbid it to speak. Until God removes the lock, the soul cannot speak of anything that happens between God and itself.

Indeed, some of the things that happen between God and the soul are reserved entirely to God himself. Satan, who goes around so anxious to know what is happening, can find no means of learning what he wants to know. So what does he do? He makes use of creatures to try to get the information he wants. And these creatures are inspired by him to praise and compliment the person concerned in such a way that they exalt that person to the third heaven, like St. Paul, to see if they can get him to fall into some vain thought or some self-satisfaction that will let Satan see what is happening in his soul.

O unforgettable Teacher, what are the wise men of this

world compared with you? Give your knowledge to all those souls who are consecrated to you so that they may be protected from the snares of Satan and may be sure of possessing you for all eternity.

Offering
To love our neighbors with a pure love for God's sake, and to love them as he commands and teaches us.

To love our neighbors for God's sake means that we must be ready in all things to serve them if they need us for anything, not considering who they are, whether they are our friends or our enemies, whether they speak well or badly of us, or whether they are grateful or ungrateful for our help. Otherwise, we are not helping them purely for God's sake, for God treats us always as well as it is possible.

The divine attribute of goodness is always doing good things for us, and yet we are very imperfect in carrying out the things relating to his holy service. But his infinite goodness continues to give us abundant graces, virtues, gifts and fruits. All he wants is to enrich us, and he rejoices and takes glory in seeing us laden with his divine treasures. He takes a kind of pride—he considers himself honored—in seeing us filled with these riches. And the more he gives us, the more his infinite goodness still wishes to give us.

So let us resolve to love our neighbor from this day on, with a pure love, for God's sake and in the way he commands and teaches us to love him.

In order to fulfill God's commandment properly, we must show this love for our neighbor, not with the affections of our heart that should be reserved for God alone, but with deeds. And we should rejoice and never mention any of our neighbor's defects, which would show that we are displeased to hear him praised or complimented. Such an attitude on our part would greatly sadden the Holy Spirit, and he would be offended.

And just as God wishes us to rejoice when we see our neighbor praised, so also he wishes us to feel sad in our heart and soul and be sorry when we see him dishonored or despised. So let us resolve from today on to follow this line of conduct toward our neighbor. In this way we shall give great pleasure and joy to God, who so rejoices when we yield the fruits of eternal life. Amen.

Consideration

The way to attain true holiness is by self-conquest and self-mortification. There is none other, nor is there any other way that will lead us more surely or more quickly to that end. For us this is very difficult, but it becomes very easy with the help we get from the Holy Spirit.

If all those people who aspire to holiness and desire it passionately realized this simple fact, then soon, very soon, they would achieve what they desire; and it is very sad to see so many souls who want to be saints who do not take the proper means to attain what they desire.

Those people meditate and pray, mentally and vocally. They fast and do great penance. They visit the sick and help the poor. They take pity on all sufferers. They receive Holy Communion with great devotion. They attend Holy Mass with great fervor. They confess all their faults with true sorrow, and not merely their sins, because people who act in this way, through the infinite mercy of God, do not commit sins—not of course that they are immune to committing them, but through the infinite mercy of God in fact they do not do so.

How is it, then, that even by living this life they do not become saints? It is simply because they fail to put into practice the most important thing of all for the achievement of holiness. For holiness is achieved by dying to oneself in all things. This death is acquired, as regards the body, by mortifying the passions, the senses and the appetites; as regards the soul, by trying to kill our self-will, our self-judgment, our vanity and all the appetites of the soul.

Once all these obstacles are overcome, it is certain, absolutely certain, that the soul will attain its sanctification. Of course, it is difficult to achieve holiness; we cannot deny that. That is to say, if we look at it from our point of view, it is very difficult; but if we regard the part God plays, then it becomes very easy.

Consider how difficult it would have been for us to grow out of our natural childhood if it had been left to ourselves. Yet this very difficult thing, which would have been so difficult if we had had to do it all by ourselves, was in fact quite easy with the help and protection of a mother given to us by God, who took care of us and continued to look after us until, by means of her help and care, we reached our full development.

What we have achieved in our natural life through the help of our mother, we achieve in the spiritual life through the care and attention with which the Holy Spirit teaches, instructs, advises, governs and defends us from all the assaults of our enemies.

Without him we have nothing and can do nothing; with him we have everything and can do everything.

He gives us all the means we need, and he teaches us, with most beautiful and graceful instructions, how to use these means. By using them properly, we may always conquer, and never be conquered, in the great battles we have to carry on. First, we must fight against ourselves, and these are the most difficult battles of all. Then we must contend against our friends and relatives and, throughout the whole of our life, against Satan, our common enemy. And as soon as we resolve to set out on the road that leads to true holiness, Satan himself comes into the battle, for in these cases he does not trust any of his assistants. Before we set out on that road, he entrusts us to them, and they carry out the work of devils very effectively. But once we determine to make holiness our goal, then he trusts no one, for the matter is too serious; he comes into the fray himself, although he can achieve nothing.

For this holy and divine SpIrit takes us into a strongly fortified castle. There, away from the world, unknown to our friends and relatives and even to ourselves, we fight and conquer, scarcely realizing what we are doing there. Because in that battle, we fight so silently, in such peace and quiet, that even the person himself who is fighting does not fully realize he is fighting and winning. There are hand-to-hand fights with Satan himself, but these come later on. Now, at the beginning, we have to train in this beautiful and fortified castle, where Satan knows nothing and can learn nothing about us, because as soon as he hears that a new soul has set out on the way to holiness he never leaves it from that moment on. He studies all its aspirations carefully, all its inclinations, desires, habits, friendships, even its devotions, everything relating to it . . . everything, for the single purpose of seducing us, deceiving us, for no other purpose than to lead us into hypocrisy and deceit.

When someone sets out on the road to holiness, Satan does not excite his passions. Before that stage he does; but as soon as we begin to live an interior life, it is the appetites he excites, and he continues to do so until the day of our death. He never gives up hope of defeating us in that way, by seducing and deceiving us with holy things, with the best things of all: with grace, with virtue, with the very holiness that we desire. That is how he gets into us. And if it were not for the Holy Spirit he would very soon defeat and completely overcome us!

But the teachings, counsels and instructions of this holy and divine Spirit keep us so well-informed of all Satan's ruses and tricks that by the time he comes to attack us, we already know what he is looking for, what he wants and everything he intends doing to us. How important, then, the Holy Spirit is for us if we are trying to attain the sanctification of our soul! And how well our divine Savior knew we would need him in everything we try to do!

That is why, when his apostles and disciples were following the Savior and he was speaking to them in that familiar way of his by means of parables and examples, seeing that he could not get them to understand the things he was saying to them, and failing to dispel their ignorance and coarseness, he said: "There is a baptism of blood, and how I long to be baptized with it!" For his heart was burning with desire to send the Holy Spirit as soon as he possibly could.

He was keeping back, as it were, cherished in his heart, that great request he wanted to make of his eternal Father, that great gift he wanted to ask for above all other gifts. And he waited until he was hanging on the Cross to ask it. It was the wisdom of the divine Word that impelled his loving heart to desire this great gift for us and that directed and governed his most holy humanity. For these two natures were so united that when Jesus Christ spoke, the divine Word spoke; therefore he knew what he was asking, and he knew when and how he should make his request in order to obtain it.

The divine Word knew well, in his infinite wisdom, that without the Holy Spirit it was of little avail that the Father should have created us or that he himself should become man and redeem us. Without the Holy Spirit we could not achieve the end for which we had been created and redeemed, for without him we are incapable of knowing Jesus Christ and much less of loving him.

Just as we cannot approach the divine Essence to enjoy it except through Jesus Christ, neither can we go to Jesus Christ except through the Holy Spirit. Therefore his divine Heart ardently burned with the desire to send him to us.

In order to show the apostles and disciples how necessary it was for him to leave them, he could find no more powerful reason than to tell them: "It is better that I go, for unless I go to the Father he cannot send you the Holy Spirit."

O divine Heart, how greatly you suffered during the three years of your public life, seeing that men were ignorant of the truth, and finding no way of making them understand you or the things you were telling them in accordance with the truth! Oh, how great is the Holy Spirit, how greatly you desired to send him to us and how greatly you had to suffer before you could do so! O holy and divine Spirit, you teach (and with every reason) all the pupils in your school to love passionately this divine Heart that loved us for thirty-three years with such an all-sacrificing love—the surest possible proof of the pure love with which that Heart has always loved us.

You constantly exhort us to love that loving Heart, wounded for love of us. That Heart seeks and desires nothing but our love in return. Its thirst can be quenched by nothing but love. It asks for nothing but love. It needs love to live; it dies for love and to be loved. O holy and divine Spirit, make more and more souls attend your school so that you can teach them to love this divine Heart which so loves us.

And we must remember that his Heart that so loves us is the heart of God who has no need of us whatever; it is we who need him.

O you souls who live an interior life, let us all unite and weave garlands of choicest myrrh and present them to the Sacred Heart of this Redeemer, which is so saddened by man's lack of love for him. Let us tell him that we will always love him with a sacrificing love and that we desire and seek nothing but that his love be the only cause of our death. Amen.

Offering

*Putting into practice the means we have
for our sanctification.*

The offering we are going to make to the Holy Spirit today is a firm resolution to put into practice all the means we have to help us attain our sanctification.

What are these means? You know them already: self-conquest and self-mortification. These are undoubtedly difficult to practice, but if we are resolved to enter completely upon an interior life, we will find that in that school where our Teacher is the Holy Spirit himself, it all becomes quite easy.

Once he sees how cowardly we are, he speaks to our soul in such a way that it immediately begins to burn with desire to undertake even the most difficult things, and with a manly spirit it starts to do battle against itself. Then with that courage which it shows in the fight, denying the appetites everything they ask, it comes out the winner in all the contests.

And look at the reward it receives for fighting and overcoming all its appetites. All who so fight and conquer are given a gratuitous and undeserved reward, a reward that is a gift of God, for the soul itself could never attain the dispositions necessary to merit it. Such is the joy we give to God by fighting and conquering in this battle that he rewards us with a great help to continue fighting and conquering, a help with which Satan is always defeated and downtrodden. And this reward that he gives us, this gift that he bestows on us, is the ability to pray without interruption, prayer that is disturbed neither by sleeping nor by recreation nor by speaking to our neighbors nor by eating nor by working, whatever our occupation may be. In fact, nothing can interrupt it. And with this prayer we acquire the intimate contact that God wants to have with our soul.

Consider, then, how well our efforts are repaid, since they are rewarded with an absolutely free reward that we could never have deserved. In this school of the Holy Spirit this prayer is called the beating of the divine Heart, because it is the continuous occupation of that loving Heart. With this prayer our divine Redeemer continuously glorified God his Father and he offered it for the salvation of the whole human race.

Let us strive, then, against ourselves until we are defeated completely so that we may obtain this gift and so that, once we obtain it, the salvation of the whole human race may be the beating of our heart also. And may our Lord and Master enter into us in friendship, and may we never lose him, so that having begun in this life, we may so continue for ever and ever. Amen.

Consideration

Let us consider the teachings and instructions that this divine Teacher gives us concerning what is the most pleasing to God and of great benefit to ourselves.

I do not intend here to tell you anything about all those immense consolations and sweetnesses that the body and soul, senses and faculties, begin to feel once they enter this school directed by such an admirable Teacher as the Holy Spirit. For to seek God for what he gives us, or for the sweetness we feel when we are with him, is a sure way of never tasting or feeling those very sweetnesses and consolations that we are seeking. Besides, it is a great obstacle and impediment to achieving union with God.

On the other hand, we achieve everything and we possess everything, because everything is given to us when we seek God alone for what he is in himself, for his own sake, and not for what he gives or has promised.

We must seek, serve, and love God unselfishly, not in order to be virtuous nor to acquire holiness or grace or even heaven itself nor for the happiness of possessing him, but solely for the sake of loving him. And when he offers us graces and gifts, we should tell him that the only gift we want is the gift of love, in order to love him. If he says to us: "Ask me for anything you like," we should ask for nothing except love and more love, in order to love him and to love him more. This is the greatest thing we can ask for or desire, because he is the only thing worth loving or desiring.

Now, once we are convinced of this fact, we can go ahead and speak of what is most pleasing to God and of great benefit to ourselves.

This most wise Teacher has such skillful ways of teaching us that they are wonderful to watch. They are all sweetness, all affection, all goodness, all prudence, all discretion.

I have said that he makes no use of words to teach, or at least very rarely. On those occasions although his voice is heard, he is not seen; but anyone who hears that voice knows that it is his. And it is heard when all the lessons he has taught have been put into practice with love and generosity.

I have already said that the lessons learned at this school must all be put into practice; otherwise, they are a waste of time and would merit only punishment. And the punishment imposed is that the school is closed down until they are put into practice. And even if we then practice them, we must still weep and be sorry with genuine sorrow for not practicing them earlier when we should have done so. He also teaches us this genuine sorrow, which is not because of the punishment or any other such interested motive. Instead, it must be heartfelt sorrow that we have failed him and because of the great displeasure we give him when our conduct forces him to punish us.

He loves us so much, so very much, and he is so sad when we force him to punish us, that he punishes us just as much for having forced him to do so as for the actual fault itself, because really we allow him no choice but to punish us. All this we understand well in the school of the Holy Spirit.

Since he is so holy and since all holiness is justice, he would not be perfect if he left unpunished, not only sin but even an imperfection. And not to be perfect would be a fault in God, and there can be no fault in him because in the infinite there is no room for fault, and God is infinite in all things.

We know all of this, not from the lessons we learn in the school, for the things I am saying now are learned simply through the close contact we have with him as our Teacher.

Everything I say now is quite true, believe me. We do not see him, but we feel him, we sense him, we taste him, we enjoy him, we feel ourselves full of him, we feel him transform our soul into himself. And all this is something the soul itself has no power to do or to attain: the Holy Spirit has to grant it as a gift. Because this divine Person is, as it were, the action of God, who comes down on us to unite us with him and to make us, through love, like a single being with him.

O true abundance, O hidden treasure, where you are, how are men to find you? They go out of themselves in search of this great treasure, while all the time it is in the center of their soul. That is where God has deposited our joy, our happiness, our rest, our consolation, our peace, our paradise on earth where we anticipate the joy and happiness of heaven. The joy we find in this school is so consoling that all the joys in the world together cannot be compared with it.

But let us leave aside those joys for the moment and continue to consider the teaching methods of this most admirable and wise Teacher.

With that bright and beautiful light which this most wise Teacher brings with him and places and leaves in our intellect, we must consider the truth that he deposits in our soul. The intellect has nothing to do but examine the truth, and it sees it perfectly with the clarity of the light that has been given it for that very purpose, and it understands it without any difficulty whatever. The intellect then communicates the truth to the will, and the will either loves it or detests and hates it, depending on what it is.

This means that if the truth in question concerns God, then the will launches out into a love of it, a love that is blind and generous. But if the truth concerns itself, then the will strives not to love it but rather to flee, detest and hate it.

Because these truths, known by the light that is given to the intellect, are all directed to knowledge of God and knowledge of self, and because the will knows that everything we see in and understand about God is worthy of being loved, then it loves it blindly and generously. And since it sees and understands perfectly that everything in itself deserves to be detested and hated, then it detests and hates it, and makes a firm resolution to strive as hard as it can until it is all rooted out.

Such is the skill of this Teacher that all his teaching brings us great joy and pleasure. Outside this school, whatever little we can do for the good of our soul is difficult for us. On the contrary, if we attend this school and persevere in it, the more we do, the more we want to do.

Once we are convinced of how important it is to kill our self-love, self-judgment and self-will, and once we put into practice the lessons taught us by this divine Teacher to achieve that object speedily, then there are no words that can adequately express the happiness the soul feels. But we can never realize what it means to be master of ourselves until we actually achieve that mastery. Apart from the possession of God himself in the blessedness of eternal glory, there is nothing greater than this self-mastery; it is paradise on earth.

With this practice and with these things killed in us, all the chains that bind us in our own slavery are broken. With this mastery, we are so happy that there is no happiness on earth that can be compared with ours. And this happiness here, which is followed by another hereafter, is the possession of God in this life through love. It is indeed a great happiness, for which I would be willing to go through every martyrdom of body and soul, because this happiness is felt, savored and enjoyed by our whole being, tasting immense riches and sweetness.

And this joy that we feel carries with it a kind of foretaste of the blessedness of eternal glory, because something shines through it, something that no words can express. It is like a mark or seal that the love of loves imprints in the most intimate part of our soul.

O you who are life, my strength, my all in all things, how well you prepare my soul with your own strength! Oh, how can anyone who receives all this still live, how can it be that he does not die, since it certainly has sufficient and excessive force within it to put an end to this natural life of ours?

How you hurt and yet heal! How near we are to death in this natural life, and yet we do not die!

O holy and divine Spirit, how I wish I had the power to get all men to live an interior life in their soul so that you would be known, desired and sought by them all. With you and with your help, your grace and your goodness, all men would attain possession of God through love in this life and ensure the blessedness of eternal glory, where they are absolutely sure of never losing him and of being able to love him without ceasing, to the fullest capacity of their love.

Offering
A firm resolution to seek nothing for ourselves that may savor of consolation, but rather to do all things merely to serve and give joy to God.

It is not easy to do things without looking for at least a little satisfaction or consolation in them, because our whole being knows and feels that we were created for joy and for joy alone. But unfortunately, as we know, our poor first parents Adam and Eve were deceived and seduced by Satan.

However, let us not regret this, because the Lord our God has redeemed us from evil, and it has all been to our immense advantage. If you begin to live an interior life, you will see the comparison between what was promised to us before and what is given to us now. So try to see what the Holy Spirit wishes and wants us to do. If you do this, you will give God very great joy and reap great advantages for yourself.

Make a firm resolution in your heart never again to commit any fault deliberately or voluntarily, and never to give to anyone or anything even the slightest affection of your heart. If you do that, then even if you feel completely dry when you try to pray, dry when you attend Mass and when you receive Communion, dry when you try to do anything, and even if the struggles the Lord asks of you are very difficult and you fight with tears in your eyes because of the strain, still you need have no fear. I for one wept often and much over this, trying to overcome myself and failing; but finally I did so.

If, when you examine yourself, you find no deliberate faults, then you have nothing to fear from this dryness. In fact, if I could meet and speak to you, I would compliment you on it, because to serve God in dryness is a definite sign that you are seeking him alone and that you are doing everything out of pure love.

All these things we learn in the divine school, where the Teacher is God himself. And who knows better than he what pleases and what displeases him, what is the best and what is not so good, what is beneficial and what is harmful to us? Who can know these things better than he?

When we are impelled to do the things relating to the service of God by the satisfaction or consolation we get in them, then, believe me, we are not seeking God and we are not doing those things for him. We are doing them out of our own self-love and we are seeking ourselves.

So let us leave the joys aside for the present: there is an eternity filled with joys awaiting us. In this life let us think only of suffering, and suffering more, for the love of him who gave his life for us. Amen.

Consideration

Let us consider the great attack that Satan prepares to launch against us when he sees us persevere in the way we have undertaken, the sufferings our soul undergoes in this fight, the great joy we give to God in the struggle and the reward he gives us for having fought, not because we deserve any reward, but out of his great love for us.

When a soul resolves to desire nothing but to follow its beloved Redeemer and to have eyes for nothing but him, determined if possible to do for him what its adorable Redeemer did and suffered for it, then Satan becomes furious. He prepares to launch a great attack, and he brings his whole infernal army with him.

And what is it he wants? What is his object? What does he hope to achieve from us with his army of followers?

Well, we learn from our unforgettable Teacher that what Satan wants is to wrench from us the three theological virtues. But he aims directly first of all at our faith, for if he can rid us of that, it will be easy for him to capture the other two, because faith is like the foundation on which the whole spiritual edifice is built, and that is what he wants to destroy. That is his object; that is what he hopes to achieve.

God then remains silent; he makes no effort to prevent Satan's attack; in fact, he even prepares the way for it. In this God also has his motives, for if the way is prepared for the Devil's attack, Satan will be all the more utterly overwhelmed, frustrated and defeated, with a most complete defeat. We, then, will be the victors in the battle and will remain invincible in the future.

When Satan launches his attack, the first thing we miss is that clear and beautiful light that God had previously given us to help us recognize the truth. Then the school closes down, and we seem to lose our memory and our reason because of the great sorrow and the sadness we feel in our soul. Poor soul, it tries to seek God, but it cannot! It wants to call out to him, but it is incapable of uttering a word. It has forgotten everything; it is in deep sorrow; it feels completely alone and isolated.

To what can I compare this state of soul? The only thing I can think of is a warm summer's night, when without any warning, heavy and horrible clouds gather overhead and hover their with their ominous darkness. We see and hear nothing but lightning that frightens us, thunder that shatters us and piercing winds that remind us of God's justice at the end of the world, like fire and brimstone that seem to be ready to destroy everything.

But really there is nothing to which I can properly compare this state. Alone, without its God, the soul feels a furious army advancing on it, shouting that the soul is mistaken, that there is no God. The army surrounds it on all sides, uttering arguments and speeches the soul does not wish to hear. This army never leaves it for a moment, always trying with loud and violent arguments to force it to believe that there is no God. With horrible browbeating, the attacking army tries to persuade the soul that the God it seeks does not exist, tries to overwhelm its faculties so that they cannot accept or believe anything but what that army is trying to compel it to accept and believe.

The soul is completely oppressed with the deepest sorrow and pain because it cannot think what awful sin it has committed to lose so completely its God and the faith it had in him. Among all those evil attackers it is so upset and dejected that it feels crushed like grapes in a wine press, as if not even a trace of faith were left in it. It becomes quite ill with such great sorrow, thinking that it has lost its God forever because it has lost its faith in him.

Then in the midst of all this immense and almost infinite pain, as if away in the distance, like something it has dreamed without realizing it has been dreaming, it remembers the Church and the love we owe it. And just like a person who has lost consciousness, and is coming to himself again and wants to speak but can only pronounce incoherent words, so the soul remembers the Church. Unable to speak, the soul stutters as if trying to say: I unite myself to all the beliefs of my mother the Church, and I want to believe nothing but what she believes.

I personally spent months and months, over a period of two years, unable to say anything more than this, unable to speak, unable to understand anything. I was eighteen at that time. And then, while I was suffering and weeping so much and so inconsolably for the loss of my faith, suddenly the bright and beautiful day dawned. Just as without realizing what was happening I had found myself in that sad state, so also when it ended I found myself being taken out of it. There I was weeping over the loss of my faith, when suddenly I saw myself beautifully arrayed in it. Now I would go through anything rather than lose that faith; and even if—although of course it is impossible—the head of the Church were to say that there is no God, I would have to say to him: God does exist, and to prove my belief, you may tear me to pieces, for I hunger and thirst to see him.

Oh, the greatness of God and the wisdom of this Teacher! Through what ways you lead me before giving me what I now have! You deprived me of the faith I had, only to give me back a faith that can never be taken from me. O my Teacher, my Teacher, who can really know you as you really are unless you yourself teach them to know you? You are wonderful in your way of teaching, and even more wonderful in the things you teach. But you are immensely more wonderful still when, on my being attacked and going into battle, you leave me alone and keep out of sight. For by doing so, you help me in my fight and allow me to end it in the most glorious triumph, leaving Satan defeated, crushed and humiliated in the sight of his followers.

I came out of that battle with a faith stronger than I ever had before. Now I can truthfully say this: My Lord, you have given me the strongest possible faith, and yet I now live without any faith because, having gone through that cruel struggle against Satan, I have been granted the gift of possessing, feeling, enjoying and holding all the things I believe. Therefore I say that after the faith has struck such deep roots in my soul, no one can take it from me. Now that you have given me such a shining faith, I live without any faith because now I have and possess what formerly I believed and hoped for. Of hope, what can I say? Have I that virtue or not? Well, I can only say that I already possess far more than I had ever hoped for.

And of charity? Oh, how my heart has increased its capacity to love! It burned with desire to love; I received love for love, and now this love that I received gives me such a hunger for more and greater love that I am burning with the desire to love God as much as I should, and yet I cannot satisfy my desire.

O my Teacher, my all in all things and in every single thing, make yourself known to all men, for they do not yet know you. At least make yourself known properly to the small group of souls that are consecrated to you. You see that those souls live with that peace, tranquillity and repose that you require in order to make your dwelling in a soul. O pure, meek, chaste and simple dove, let them feel the amorous cooing of your chaste love, and they will remain forever in love with and absorbed in you.

Remember, O supreme goodness, that the Creator

gave us a heart to love with and be loved, yet we waste it in false, deceitful and petty loves. Teach us to love as you love, with a love that is pure, chaste, unselfish, strong, sweet, lovable, consoling, constant and enduring. Give us a love like your love, a love that grows and increases every day, that not even death dissolves, for it goes on to eternity. Through all eternity it increases and, thus increasing, loves for ever and ever, as long as you continue to exist. And we know that you will reign for all eternity because eternity came from you, from the life that you have always lived in immense love, and with that love you love all those who wish you to love them. O my goodness and sweetness, make them understand all this.

Lead the minds of all men out of their vast ignorance, enlighten them with your bright and beautiful light, and let them see with that light how infinite and boundless is your love. Teach them to seek, wish and desire no other love but yours and to respond generously to the love you have for them. Heaven of heavens, let me enjoy the consolation of seeing you soon known and loved by all your creatures.

Oh, how great it will be to see you for ever and ever prolong the endless eternity into the limitless future for those who have sought, served and loved you. To see you prolong them in measureless love, the purest and most delightful love, which is that which springs from the purity and holiness of God, the divine Essence, and from the divine perfections that are comprised in him. And how great it will be to enjoy those perfections in such a way that no one can hinder, disturb or diminish our enjoyment of them, but they will only increase for ever and ever.

Oh, what a life that will be! Lord, here I am praying to you. You know what I want to ask of you: grant that the loving plans you have for all your creatures be fulfilled in this life so that they may live with you for ever and ever in the next. Amen.

Offering
Confidence in God.

The offering we are going to make to the Holy Spirit today is a resolution never to lose confidence in God or to allow ourselves to become despondent, for that is the path by which Satan leads many souls to despair.

Never allow despondency or lack of confidence to enter your soul. Look at Judas, and see the end he came to because he lost hope; look at Peter, and see what he became through confidence in God.

Why did our sweet Lord Jesus call Judas his friend, and he called none of the others by that name? It was to encourage him to have confidence in him. If Judas, even at the moment when the Lord called him his friend, had only acknowledged and repented of his sin, do you think he would have despaired and been condemned? He would not.

Our unforgettable Teacher, speaking of the enormity of the error we commit if we lose confidence in him, tells us that if Judas had gone to Jesus Christ, confident that he would forgive him his sin, not only would he have forgiven him, but he would have regarded him as a friend forever after, and would have shown him through deeds that they were really friends. But Christ alone could not save him because, as we are told by this most wise Teacher, God who created us without our cooperation will not save us without our cooperation.

This is yet another proof of the love he has for us, which he shows us in this way. For God knows well how clever Satan is and how he strives to get us to lose confidence in God and not go to him when we sin and offend him just as when we please and satisfy him in all things. What, then, does God want us to do? He wants us always to go to him with perfect confidence.

Do you think that God loves us less than our mother? Believe me, he always looks on us as children because in relation to him we always act as children.

How often when we were children our mother would warn us: Don't do that or you'll hurt yourself? If you do that, I will slap you? And yet we went ahead and did that very thing, and everything turned out exactly as she had warned us. Then we would cry and shout and continue crying: Mother, Mother. And if we had hurt ourselves seriously, we came running to her, trusting neither ourselves nor our friends or neighbors or relatives, because we knew that our mother loved us more than anyone else.

So it happens also in the spiritual life. Even though she may punish us and we know that she may do so, yet we cry for our mother. And what does she do then? She does not think of punishing us, because she sees the serious hurt we have done ourselves and her only concern is to cure us. And in her loving way she shows us how much she loves us and how sorry she feels for our pain.

So if Judas, instead of losing hope and giving in to despair, had called out to God for pardon, like a child calling his mother, then God, who has a more loving heart than any mother, would have given him his grace and his help to come to repentance and sorrow, and everything would have been settled: God would have been satisfied and Judas would have returned to his friendship and grace. But how sad Christ was to see that Judas did not behave in this way!

Let us not make him sad in this way. Let us not also lose confidence in him and become despondent. Let us always call on him whenever we commit imperfections, faults or even serious sins. For with his grace and help he cures all our ills and we are as perfectly cured as if nothing whatever had happened to us. And if we behave always in this way, we can be sure that we will possess God for ever and ever. Amen.

Consideration

Let us consider the final attack that Satan launches against the soul. It is the most cunning attack that all his knowledge and malice could invent, for its object is to rob God of what is rightfully his and to fill the soul with pride, thereby separating it from God forever.

When Satan sees that all his efforts to deprive the soul of its faith have been in vain, he begins to wonder whether God has intervened in the fight against him. Once he suspects this, he resolves to give up fighting against us directly, either himself or any of his followers, but rather to try to get his work done for him by the people who come in contact with us. He even tries to enlist the aid of our confessor, not getting him to speak of our sins, of course, because the priest would let himself be killed rather than disclose any sin of ours. But since he may speak openly of anything except our sins, that is what Satan tries to get him to do. The people of the world around us, then, prompted by Satan, begin to speak of us with neither truth nor foundation, some saying that we do great penance, others saying that we have ecstasies, revelations or visions, and others that God loves and favors us in special ways, and many other things of this nature.

And just as everyone knows there is a fire when they hear the fire alarm even in the distance, and they soon know where it is, so people are prompted by Satan to hear and think things that are untrue. This is all Satan's invention. It is of no importance to him that what they say is untrue provided it helps him to achieve his purpose. The thing is that they say and spread such things about a person that people think that person is a saint. And from then on he is called and regarded as such.

Poor soul. What would happen to you in this situation if it were not for the lessons you have seen and learned in the divine school? There you are presented with God himself as a mirror in which to look at yourself and to keep looking until you get to know and see yourself as you really are. What would happen to you, poor child of Adam, if you had not been truthfully shown beforehand the ruses that Satan would use against you, and all his evil intentions? How would you have escaped from his clutches, with all the knowledge and power he has? Remember that God left him all those faculties, and he uses them now so astutely and maliciously to seduce and deceive you.

You are indeed blessed, O divine light, and a thousand times blessed. For through your brightness I came to know God, who is supreme greatness, perfect holiness, fount and source of all perfection, unchanging truth, infinite power, true life. Through him I shall never lose it, for it was he who gave me the true life of my soul that I now have and live. And if there is anything in me that is not sin, it is from him; and if there is anything in me that is worthy of praise, it was he who gave it to me. I received everything from him; I have nothing of my own because I am nothingness itself. I came from dust, and dust is my whole inheritance. None but God alone deserves praise, and cursed is he who praises anyone else but him alone, for he is the only thing that exists worthy of praise.

How miserable we are when your supernatural light ceases to enlighten our mind! We are robbers and thieves, for we rob you of the praise that is rightfully yours and we give it to poor creatures. We are blind, for we cannot see the truth. We are ignorant, for we do not know where the truth is or where we seek it. We are stupid, for it is stupid, and very stupid, to think that a poor creature is whatever people say he is, when if left to himself he cannot take even one step in the right direction or make even one move toward holiness. We are senseless, for what greater nonsense can there be than this: we see that the infinite goodness of God covers the poverty of his creatures in his own virtues, and adorns their misery and vileness with his gifts and favors, and yet instead of exalting and praising the infinite goodness that bestows these things, we praise the poor creatures who receive them? Surely this is completely senseless! And when you praise someone for fasting and doing penance and say that he is a saint because he does them, how can you know whether he is acting in those things with the purity of intention he should have, whether he omits to give God the honor he asks of him, whether he is even doing things he should not do at all, or whether he is doing things in order to be praised for it? In all these cases God is greatly displeased, and yet you say the person is a saint!

Do you think God is satisfied with merely external things, as we are? Try to understand that true holiness is not so much on the outside; rather, it is inside, deep inside. That is where God has placed it and that is where he wants us to seek it, for only there can it be found, and only by what is there inside can holiness be judged. So you see how difficult it is to recognize holiness! It is hidden away in the innermost part of the heart and soul. And who can know what is in there except God and the person's own understanding, which sees what God approves and reproves? No one else can enter there. God has decreed, in his infinite and uncreated wisdom, that no one can penetrate those innermost parts except God and the soul itself and that in there, without the sound of any words, those two should be able to speak secretly and understand each other.

And in this matter, what God has decreed is fulfilled to the letter. So why do people insist on praising others when they know so little about them? Who prompts them to do so? No one but Satan himself.

Because Satan wishes to deprive God of the joy he takes in loving and being loved by men, now he is actually the most useful and most opportune instrument that God has for shaping, forming and polishing all the genuine saints.

How is it that Satan never learns from all the defeats he has suffered? And yet we cannot expect him to learn anything, since pride, revenge and envy are, so to speak, his very life! Rage is an evil that is never got rid of; it persists until death. And since Satan cannot die, he has to go on living always, and he lives in rage and despair. Since he has so much power and wisdom, and yet is so malicious and vindictive, such a liar and such a traitor, he is fully convinced that he will deceive us in one way or another.

Meanwhile God, who has dominion over all the powers of hell, remains silent and lets him carry on as he wishes. And then, when Satan and all his army have everything prepared, the soul, with God, defeats them all and leaves them confounded and in disgrace.

So although Satan does not realize it, in fact he contributes to make the soul, which is in love with its God, love him even more, and to make God be more pleased than ever with the soul and love it still more. And, again through the intervention of Satan, once the battle is over, the soul reaches a state that it would perhaps never have reached otherwise, but that now it has been given as a reward for the fight, the battle, the combat it has waged against Satan.

O God invincible in battles, O unforgettable Teacher, what divine ways you have of teaching the soul and then of making it see and feel through its own experience the very things your immense wisdom has taught it!

But the greatest, the most beautiful, most consoling and most satisfying thing of all is to see you conquer without fighting, and defeat without destroying, without being seen, heard or felt by your enemies. Peace, tranquillity, calm and quiet—these are the weapons you teach us to use so well and by using them to destroy those who come to fight against us. Make us fight always with these weapons so that we may first conquer ourselves and then, after that triumph, defeat Satan and put him to shame. Amen.

Offering
Doing all things in truth.

This offering, which will be pleasing to the Holy Spirit, is a firm resolution to do all things in truth and with truth, and in the way that God wants us to do them. And one of these things that we should do in truth and with truth is to be careful neither to praise nor condemn, neither to desire nor reject, unless we first see the truth in the matter.

To praise truthfully is to praise the saints who have been beatified by the Church. This is what God wishes and it is very pleasing to him. But to praise people who are living among us when we see they are favored by God—this is not to praise according to the truth. If we want to praise the good we see in someone, then let us praise God who gave it to him rather than praising him who only received it.

In this matter, we should act as we would if we saw a poor man dressed through the charity of a rich benefactor, for in that case we would all say: Look at the suit and all the clothes that poor man is wearing; they were given to him by so-and-so (naming the charitable benefactor). And in that we would act according to the truth. But if, instead of praising him who gave, we praised him who received, any intelligent or sensible person would say to us, and quite rightly: Surely you should praise the person who gave him those clothes and not the poor man who only received them. Surely you see that what you are saying is not right and therefore should not be said.

Neither should we be upset when we ourselves are condemned, nor should we desire to be praised, for in that there would be no truth either.

Let us try to realize that if we see someone do something well and reasonably and we praise that person or regard him as a saint, then we are doing Satan's work. The fact is that we all, children of Adam, have a tendency to be vain; it is ingrained in us, and we must do our best to get rid of it. You can see how true this is of everyone: you will seldom lose anyone's friendship by praising him! If you say to someone who you think is ill: You are not looking well, I have noticed this thing and that other thing about you, and they are symptoms of illness, he will not be offended. But the moment you point out any defect in him, then you will see whether he continues to be a friend of yours! And if we want to praise someone, then let us praise God, for it is he who gives us everything good we have, and in that way we shall be doing something very pleasing to the Holy Spirit. Amen.

THE TENTH DAY

Consideration

If the soul puts into practice all it is taught in this divine school where the Teacher is the Holy Spirit, then it will neither walk nor run nor fly along the way of holiness; instead, it will advance with the speed and agility with which our thoughts can skip from one place to another.

In this school, directed by the Holy Spirit in the center of our soul, the subject we learn is far above all human subjects. And there are two books used in this school. The first, which we pupils use, has two parts, and the name of the book is *The Humanity of Our Adorable Redeemer.*

The first part comprises all the external acts performed by Jesus Christ, our divine Redeemer. We study it and continue to study it until we have imprinted it on our memory like a picture, so that always and in all things we may live in his presence. If we reach that stage, our Teacher tells us that this is sufficient.

The second part of this first book consists of practicing its contents. When it comes to the question of practice, each person has to act according to his strength and ability. In this school, although we all have to practice the same things, our Teacher is so prudent and discreet, so merciful and compassionate, that he never demands of us more than each one can give, and he wants each of us to read the book for himself and to do what he finds written there. For although this holy humanity of our Redeemer is the open book for all of us to read, which we have to learn and put into practice, nevertheless, our unforgettable Teacher explains to us that he is the great architect who plans, designs and constructs the buildings of our souls very differently one from another. While he uses the same cement and the same materials in them all, there is yet immense variety in his ways of shaping and forming them. For he builds some with only one story, and some with two or more, while others he builds to very great heights. Some he paints and makes beautiful inside, leaving them plain on the outside; others he makes beautiful both inside and out. Some he builds in places where there is no one to know or see them, and others he places in the open for everyone to see and admire. He does all things as his great wisdom plans, designs and disposes.

What he wishes, then, is that whenever we see one of the pupils of this school being raised by God to great heights while we are left where we are, we should help him and join with him in giving thanks to God for having deigned to glance at him. But we should never praise or exalt the person himself, because we cannot know whether in fact he deserves praise for what he has or contempt for what he does.

We cannot see what goes on in the heart or soul of another, and this is the only thing that matters to God, the only thing that pleases or displeases him. And no one but God can enter into anyone's heart or soul.

So let each of us judge for himself how much he pleases or displeases God. Let us try to see deeply into the life of Jesus Christ, to see what went on in that blessed soul and that loving heart, how they acted, and the disposition and purpose they had in all their actions, so that we also may act in all things for the same purpose as our Redeemer. And we see and learn all this very well in the second part of the first book, which is the only one we should work at.

The second book used in this school is at the disposal only of the Teacher. He does not teach it to us, because this book and everything it contains is far above the understanding of any human intelligence. And how is he to give us a true and clear idea of how incomprehensible this book is? Well, as he is so wise, so powerful and so subtle in all his teaching methods, once we reach the end of the practice contained in the second part of the first book, as if to reward our diligence in putting into practice all we have learned in it, he speaks to us intimately and tells us that the other book, which is so far beyond our understanding, is called *God, the Divine Essence.* Then immediately the soul feels itself with all its faculties being carried away and lifted up by some superior force outside itself, which it does not understand. And it is raised high above all created things, not only on earth but also in what people call the firmament and we call heaven, that is to say the house or palace, or whatever we may like to call it, where God placed his angels when he created them.

Above and beyond these heavens, up to immense and limitless heights, my soul was transported by a mysterious force. With the subtlety of our thoughts, which can in the twinkling of an eye go from one end of the earth to the other, with that same speed I found myself carried up there, to those immense and limitless heights. I found myself up there where God has his imperial palace, in those heavens that always existed, since they are, so to speak, the throne of God.

How am I to express what is experienced in those regions, when the soul is so carried away by the sight of so much beauty that it can say nothing? All those who are there rejoicing in God see one another, look at one another and congratulate one another. But there is no word spoken, for they have a divine language, through which they all understand one another by looking at one another in God, and are all carried away and glorify God. They move about in those limitless heavens with that agility which they always have, and yet they are always, so to speak, immersed in the center of God, wherever they go, however much they move. They are always in the center of God and always enraptured by his divine beauty and magnificence. For he is an immense ocean of wonders, and an essence constantly flowing and pouring itself out.

And since what pours out from God is his greatness and beauty, his happiness, blessedness and everything else that is in him, the soul is always immersed in the happiness, blessedness and glory that emanate from God.

God is heaven prolonged, and therefore the soul is forever finding and rejoicing in new heavens, each filled with inconceivable beauty and loveliness. All this beauty and loveliness are always enjoyed by the soul while immersed in God. And moving about in these new and spacious heavens, the soul is eternally happy.

It is quite impossible to give an adequate description of this state. If the cherubim all came down on earth and began to speak, even with the wonderful intelligence God has given them and with the sincere desire they all feel to make God and all his works known, even they could tell us nothing and could give us no proper idea of what the heavens involve. And who can speak to us adequately or tell us anything clearly about God? For he has no body, no shape, no appearance. Who, then, can tell us what he is like? How could we describe this perfection of every perfection, this perfection of every beauty, when we can scarcely give a clear description of many things we do in fact see and feel? For instance, can you describe clarity for me? Or a beautiful dawn? Or our life? Or all the flowers, plants and other living things?

O life always lived, you who are the only living life, my God and my all: who can speak to us about you or tell us what you are?

Since anyone who sees you is carried away and out of himself to such an extent that he cannot even tell whether he is alive or dead, because just the thought of you transports him and makes him lose himself completely, who then can tell us anything about you?

There is no comparison whatever between the knowledge of God we acquire in this divine school and the knowledge we had of him before. It is as if a man born blind, who knows what nature is merely through what others have told him of it, were suddenly to lose his blindness and see nature face to face, as it really is. Perhaps such a man could tell us the difference between the reality as he sees it and what he has been told of it by others.

So, O my Teacher, take us all into your school so that, like the blind man, we may see what you are, for no one else can describe you to us. How can we expect any creature to be able to do so, since from their very beginning they are nothing? How can they explain something whose immense greatness and great majesty are quite incomprehensible? There is no intelligence, whether human or angelic, however great it be, capable of describing it to us, for all greatness except the greatness of God has a limit and once we reach that limit we can go no further. Who, then, can speak to us of God and tell us what he is?

No one, no one, either in heaven or on earth. For God is the furnace of eternal light, shining in immense brilliance, the source of all perfections radiating every virtue. Each one of his infinite perfections has its own mode of being, and by its nature is infinite in beauty and elegance. Each one is so overwhelming that anyone who sets eyes on it is overcome, taken out of himself and absorbed in its beauty and loveliness, and feels himself immersed in that beauty and loveliness. And they in turn again make him feel himself overcome, taken out of himself and absorbed by the immense happiness and blessedness that the soul feels within itself.

And the immense happiness and blessedness are felt at the mere sight of any one of God's infinite perfections.

What, then, will the soul not feel at the sight of all his perfections and virtues and attributes together?

And just think what it will be like when we see ourselves
loved by God in the sight of all angels and all men, with a
love such as God's, which is like no other love. It leaves the
soul intoxicated with happiness, fills it to the brim and
leaves nothing else for it to desire! For God's love brings to
the soul and to the body all kinds of abundance of happiness, blessedness and glory; and it never ceases to love us
and its love never diminishes for the whole of eternity.

Consider what the soul will feel when it finds itself so
loved for all eternity by him who is the only thing that is.
And who can describe or tell us what the soul will feel
merely by looking at him when the sight of him leaves the
soul submerged as if in immense oceans, bottomless seas,
heavens that are limitless and without end? For all this is
what the divine Essence contains.

Who can describe God to us, when no one can express
even what we feel merely by looking at him? Then the soul
is deified and left without any life in itself and lives only
in God. So what can it tell us, since it is thus deified, absorbed, overwhelmed and wrenched out of itself by its
overabundance of happiness?

No one can utter a word when he is so overwhelmed.
Even if he could speak, how could he express something
so completely above all our understanding? And if this is
the effect of merely seeing God, what will the soul not feel
when God gives himself over to it, to possess him and rejoice in him forever? If he produces these effects in a soul
that merely sees him, what joy will the soul not feel when
it actually possesses him? How infinite God must be in
himself!

O supreme greatness, O you who always live with your
own life, and who gave life to all living things, how I wish
I had, now in this present life, an infinite capacity for

rejoicing, so that I could rejoice infinitely in your being who you are!

And yet men deny your existence, you who are the only thing that is or that lives with a life of its own! O my all in all things, speak and make yourself felt from one end of the earth to the other. Tell all creatures that you have no need of them, that if you desire them, it is solely in order to cure their ills, to rid them of their pettiness and misery, and to give them the happiness and blessedness they are seeking and cannot find because those exist only in you, who are the fount and source of all happiness and blessedness. And how are they to seek them in you when they do not believe in you and deny your existence?

Come, O holy and divine Spirit, come down on earth. Strike all men in such a way that they will no longer resist your divine call but will leave behind them those childish things that now occupy them. Those things are another ruse by which Satan wins over men's hearts in such a way that, seduced and cheated, they spend their life distracted by childish things. So death catches them and they fail to achieve the very end for which they were created.

O holy and divine Spirit, do not abandon us to these useless occupations. Use the power that as God you possess and compel us to go to you. Carry out your loving plans in all of us, so that we will all praise, exalt and glorify you and rejoice in your divine goodness, so that we will all live by you and be deified in your divine presence for ever and ever. Such was your plan and desire for us even before we existed. Amen.

Offering
The three theological virtues.

Today we are going to promise the Holy Spirit to keep, preserve and protect these divine virtues, so as never to lose them. There is no creature who knows as well as Satan the value of these three virtues. That is why he goes around like a hunter, never tiring in his search, to see if any of them will fall prey to him. He is immensely pleased with himself when he finds a prey in any one of them, for he prowls in search of them one at a time.

If he catches one, he has the three almost within his grasp. Faith, of course, is his main target, for if he manages to injure this one he is sure of the other two also, because any injury to faith is fatal. But if his infernal arrow strikes hope or charity he is not quite so pleased with himself, because these wounds are easily healed; if he strikes faith, it is a mortal wound, and then how delighted he is!

These three virtues together form, as it were, one tree. The root and trunk are faith; the branches are hope; the fruits are charity. If he cuts the branches, then the tree remains without branches or fruit; but it still lives, because the root and the tree can soon sprout new branches, and these will give new fruit. But if he takes away the trunk and the root, then the tree disappears, because once the trunk and the root are gone, the branches and fruit die.

Those who are consecrated to God in the solitude of their cloisters attach great importance and esteem to what are called visions and revelations. But what should be esteemed more is one act of faith. We should believe firmly in those visions and revelations that God has revealed to his Church and that the Church approves, but in no others.

If we act in this way, we shall give the Holy Spirit great consolation. Amen.

POSTSCRIPTS

I.

I ask you to accept this little book as a token of the esteem and admiration I have for you. And I admire and esteem you very much because you have been chosen by Jesus Christ, our divine Redeemer. Strive to enter this divine school, where we are taught to live and act as children of such a holy Father, as spouses of such a sweet Lord and as pupils of such a holy and unforgettable Teacher.

What great things the most august Trinity has prepared to give us on that day when we shall go to the paternal house to celebrate our longed-for union, in a celebration that will last for ever and ever!

Accept this expression of the affection I feel for you in the Father who created us, in the divine Word who redeemed us and in the Holy Spirit our sanctifier, to whom in the unity of the most Blessed Trinity be all praise, all honor and all glory for ever and ever. Amen.

II.

PRIZES AWARDED IN THIS SCHOOL
OF DEVOTION TO THE HOLY SPIRIT

These prizes are not earned or merited, but are awarded to us out of the pure goodness of our unforgettable Teacher, the Holy Spirit.

Although they are bestowed directly on the faculties of the soul, our whole being feels the great happiness they bring with them, because they are recreation and pleasure for the body, and anticipation of heaven for the soul.

Prizes awarded to the memory
This faculty is allowed to make trips, without any effort on its part, to Bethlehem, Egypt and Jerusalem, to follow Jesus Christ in his public life, to accompany him to Tabor where he was transfigured, to the Garden of Olives, to the praetorium, through the streets of Jerusalem and to Calvary, to enjoy a loving picture of our adorable Redeemer whenever it wishes.

Prizes awarded to the understanding
This faculty is granted knowledge of the divine Essence and the three divine Persons, this knowledge being accommodated to the capacity of our human understanding; also knowledge of the creation of angels and of man, of the angels' rebellion, disobedience and punishment, of the Incarnation of the divine Word.

Prizes awarded to the will
This faculty is embraced by that most passionate and most refined of all lovers, and blessed with arrow wounds of divine love deep in the soul. The soul is transformed in God and enjoys most tender and loving delights. As a child sweetly reposing in its mother's arms and at the same time being nourished with milk, so is the soul nourished here, with wisdom and knowledge and possession of the most Blessed Trinity.

> *A thousand lives, if they were mine,*
> *Would I give but to possess you;*
> *A thousand? . . . many, many more*
> *To love you, if I could love you*
> *With that same pure, strong love*
> *With which you, my love, who are you,*
> *Love us for ever and ever.*